T0323597

Cambridge Elements ≡

Elements in Intercultural Communication
edited by
Will Baker
University of Southampton
Troy McConachy
University of New South Wales
Sonia Morán Panero
University of Southampton

INTERCULTURAL COMMUNICATION IN VIRTUAL EXCHANGE

Francesca Helm
University of Padova

CAMBRIDGE
UNIVERSITY PRESS

CAMBRIDGE
UNIVERSITY PRESS

Shaftesbury Road, Cambridge CB2 8EA, United Kingdom

One Liberty Plaza, 20th Floor, New York, NY 10006, USA

477 Williamstown Road, Port Melbourne, VIC 3207, Australia

314–321, 3rd Floor, Plot 3, Splendor Forum, Jasola District Centre, New Delhi – 110025, India

103 Penang Road, #05-06/07, Visioncrest Commercial, Singapore 238467

Cambridge University Press is part of Cambridge University Press & Assessment, a department of the University of Cambridge.

We share the University's mission to contribute to society through the pursuit of education, learning and research at the highest international levels of excellence.

www.cambridge.org
Information on this title: www.cambridge.org/9781009572002

DOI: 10.1017/9781009385589

When citing this work, please include a reference to the DOI 10.1017/9781009385589

First published 2024

A catalogue record for this publication is available from the British Library.

ISBN 978-1-009-57200-2 Hardback
ISBN 978-1-009-38557-2 Paperback
ISSN 2752-5589 (online)
ISSN 2752-5570 (print)

Intercultural Communication in Virtual Exchange

Elements in Intercultural Communication

DOI: 10.1017/9781009385589
First published online: December 2024

Francesca Helm
University of Padova

Author for correspondence: Francesca Helm, francesca.helm@unipd.it

Abstract: Virtual exchange is an educational approach that uses technology to bring together people from geographically and/or culturally distant locations in sustained online interactions, often intended to develop their intercultural awareness and understanding. Though the practice has existed for several decades, it has gained popularity in recent years, in part due to the recent Covid-19 pandemic and recourse to online tools for international and intercultural learning. This Element explores intercultural communication in virtual exchange by looking at how and why culture is made relevant in the pedagogical design and framing of virtual exchanges and what impact this might have on student positioning, power dynamics, and on intercultural learning. From this framework three broad approaches are outlined, which are defined as comparative, challenge-based, and dialogue-based. Each approach is explored through examples and the opportunities, limitations, and risks for intercultural learning.

This Element also has a video abstract: www.cambridge.org/EIIC-Helm

Keywords: virtual exchange, intercultural communication, internationalisation at home, COIL (collaborative online international learning), telecollaboration

ISBNs: 9781009572002 (HB), 9781009385572 (PB), 9781009385589 (OC)
ISSNs: 2752-5589 (online), 2752-5570 (print)

Contents

Introduction

We are living in paradoxical times. Great efforts and resources are being invested by companies, universities, and research centres to make technologies more human, so they can interact *with* humans *like* humans. We see this, for example, in the use of chatbots as teaching assistants (Kim et al., 2020). The growth of artificial intelligence no doubt has many implications for education, yet what many seem to be ignoring is how we can also use online technologies to foster engagement and interaction with *real* humans across geographic/political/social/cultural divides. Today we are surrounded by increasing nationalism and populism that create divisions, racist discourses and practices that posit certain people as less than human and less worthy of living than others. The need to create spaces and collaborations in our education systems that serve to humanise the 'other' is more important than ever. This Element is about virtual exchange (VE), an educational approach which can open up possibilities for creating such spaces for intercultural communication through online technologies. The practice of connecting students and classrooms online is not something new, it began in the 1990s (Warschauer, 1995). More recently it has come to be recognised and valued as a form of 'internationalisation at home' (Beelen & Jones, 2015; O'Dowd, 2023), offering students international and intercultural experiences that are more accessible than physical mobility. Virtual exchange also holds potential, I believe, for challenging the predominantly neoliberal approach to internationalisation that Marginson (2022) argues has colonised the globalisation of higher education by transforming it into a competitive global marketplace characterised by the cultural linguistic monoculture of Anglo-American knowledge.

This Element stems from my experience as a language educator and researcher in the global north who started dabbling with the use of technologies in my teaching to offer students opportunities to use English for what I then saw as 'authentic communication' with 'native speakers' of the language. This was almost thirty years ago and since then much has changed in terms of technologies and global interconnectedness – and also theorising in my areas of study, applied linguistics and intercultural communication. The construct of the 'native speaker' as an ideal interlocutor and a model that language learners should aspire to has been challenged on many fronts (Baker, 2015; Ortega & Zyzik, 2008; Phillipson, 1992; Train, 2006) and has been replaced by the 'intercultural speaker' (Byram, 1997). Understandings of languages and cultures as static bounded entities have been superseded by a recognition of the fluid nature of language, culture, and identity. We are called upon to identify, interrogate, and interrupt coloniality (Souza, 2019) and recognise that 'all cultures, languages, and knowledges are incomplete and in a constant process of becoming through interaction/relations with others' (Souza & Duboc, 2021, p. 886).

This Element focuses on intercultural communication in VE, not only in language education but in various fields, including business, teacher education, history and political science, peacebuilding, and global citizenship education. It begins with a definition of VE, a brief history of how the field has developed over the last three decades, and an overview of different models of VE. Section 2 briefly reviews some of the key approaches and concerns in the field of intercultural communication and outlines the interdiscursive approach taken in this Element, that is, looking at *how* and *why* culture is made relevant in the pedagogical design and framing of a VE.

The key questions that I ask are:

- How is culture made relevant in the pedagogical design/context of a VE?
- What impact might this have on student positioning within the exchange and on intercultural learning?
- What are the opportunities for learning in this approach to culture and intercultural communication, and what are the limitations or risks?

This theoretical frame is then applied in the following sections that focus on what I have identified as three different conceptualisations of culture and intercultural communication in VE: comparative, challenge-based, and dialogue-based. In each of these sections, I present selected VEs as models and examples of the approach and discuss the opportunities and limitations they offer, drawing on published research findings. I also draw attention to the dominance of Western/Northern epistemologies in these approaches and the risk of reproducing of colonial dynamics. The Element concludes by briefly reviewing the three approaches to VE and the ways in which they can and sometimes do overlap, and a call for 'practice with conceptual reflection' (Souza & Duboc, 2021).

1 What Is Virtual Exchange?

Virtual exchange (VE) is an umbrella term that defines educational practices or approaches that use online technologies to bring together students situated in different geographical locations and/or from different cultural backgrounds in order to foster intercultural and/or disciplinary learning through sustained inter-action and/or collaboration with their distant peers (Helm, 2018a; O'Dowd 2023). The term has become widely used since the late 2010s and refers to a range of practices, also known as telecollaboration, online intercultural exchange, globally networked learning, and COIL (collaborative online international learning), which have developed in various educational and disciplinary contexts (see O'Dowd 2018, for a discussion on the terminology). Virtual exchange has been adopted above all in foreign language education, business, and management, and increasingly in other areas such as teacher education, STEM, health sciences, and global citizenship education (O'Dowd, 2023; Stevens Initiative, 2024). It has been conceptualised as a *pedagogic approach* offering students *experiential* intercultural learning; a *tool* for 'internationalisation at home'; an online *environment* or *context* designed for students to engage in intercultural communication and translocal collaborations, a *safe/brave space* as a 'springboard to engage collaboratively with complexity' (Glimäng, 2022, p. 78) and a *Thirdspace* for thinking 'otherwise', that is, as 'an alternative for decolonial, non-dominant, borderless, collaborative forms of learning' (Guimarães & Finardi, 2021, p. 5).

The term 'virtual' is somewhat unfortunate, as it suggests that something is not 'real' (see Colpaert, 2020, and O'Dowd, 2021, for a discussion), though of course, the online world is very much part of the daily lives of many people – so much so that scholars are beginning to argue that it is futile to distinguish between the two (Bagga-Gupta & Dahlberg, 2021; Dovchin et al., 2018). The conversations we have, and relations developed online can become friendships in the 'real' world, and many of our 'real life' family relations are maintained predominantly through so-called virtual interactions. Yet, as Kern (2014) reminds us, 'the medium matters' (p. 97). Technologies and the way we use them, both as individuals and also broader groups, *do* have an impact on our relations and communications so should be taken into account when discussing online intercultural interactions and pedagogies (Helm, 2018a). The term 'exchange' is also important in VE and distinguishes it from other terms such as 'virtual mobility' and 'virtual learning' (O'Dowd, 2023). It highlights that VE is not about the unidirectional transmission of content and knowledge through online tools, but rather about creating opportunities for an exchange of perspectives, experiences, knowledges through interaction, collaboration, dialogue, and listening. Yet the meaning of exchange too can be reduced to mean mere transactions. Virtual exchange is, or at least I believe should be, based on values of reciprocity, mutual learning, and relational learning, which is defined by Icaza and Vázquez (2018) as follows:

> A relational approach is not simply a participatory approach, a relational approach is one in which the diverse backgrounds and the geo-historical positioning of the different participants in the classroom are rendered valuable in a dignified way for the learning of all. Practices of teaching and learning that are grounded in relational approaches or democratic forms of teaching can contribute to decolonising our forms of learning. (p. 120)

1.1 Origins of Virtual Exchange

The Covid-19 pandemic led to a surge of interest in VE, partly due to the total, albeit temporary, halt to international student mobility, but VE is not a new pedagogic practice. The foundations of VE lie in collaborative educational programmes that sought to make contacts outside of the classroom through uses of technologies. Often cited in the VE literature are French educator Célestin Freinet working in France in the 1920s and Mario Lodi working in Italy in the 1960s, whose project-based learning, class newspapers, and exchange of documents and cultural packages opened up their classes to distant peers (O'Dowd, 2023). These were born well before the emergence of online technologies and used analogue technologies such as pen and paper, and the printing press.

One of the earliest known exchange projects which used online technologies to connect distant classes in schools was the New York/Moscow Schools Telecommunications Project, launched in 1988 (Helm, 2018b; Uvarov & Prussakova, 1992). This project was a response to a perceived need to connect youth from the United States and the USSR during a time marked by the tensions that had developed during the Cold War. The pilot project, between twelve schools in each nation, was supported by the Sciences in Moscow Academy and the New York State Board of Education. Students worked in both English and Russian on projects based on their curricula, which had been designed by participating teachers. The project was based on the assumption that 'the problems facing the world are created by people, either individually or collectively, and that these problems can be resolved through effective communication' (Magi Educational Services, 1992, p. 3). This exchange was further developed by iEARN[1] (the international Education and Resource Network), an NGO in the United States, who expanded it in the early 1990s to include China, Israel, Australia, Spain, Canada, Argentina, and the Netherlands. iEARN began to develop other projects, such as Learning Circles[2] and the Orillas project[3] (Cummins & Sayers, 1997) to build partnerships with educators across the globe. The power of these exchanges was seen in their potential to increase intercultural communications and cooperation and, according to Cummins and Sayers (1997), they presented a powerful alternative to the directions that educational reform in the United States was taking at the time. In their view, these types of online intercultural collaborations derived their impact not from technology, but from 'a vision of how education can enact, in a microcosm, a radical restructuring of power relations both in domestic and global arenas' (1997, p. 8). The Learning Circles and Orillas projects continue to run today, as well as many other projects connecting schools across the globe through iEARN.

---

[1] www.iearn.org/. [2] www.globallearningcircles.org/. [3] www.orillas.org/.

In a slightly later and somewhat different historical and geopolitical context, but with a similar vision to iEARN, the Soliya Connect Program[4] was developed in 2003. Just two years after 9/11 and the beginning of George Bush's 'War on Terror', Soliya's Connect Program (which will be discussed in Section 5) was designed to address the tensions between 'Western' and 'predominantly Arab and Muslim' societies. The main focus of the project was to connect students from these two regions and seek to have an impact on the development of empathy, cross-cultural communication skills, critical thinking, and activation, that is, pursuing further opportunities for such engagement (Himelfarb & Idriss, 2011).

In higher education institutions, it was above all in foreign language teaching that VE, then known as 'telecollaboration' emerged in the 1990s. Online technologies were seen as presenting opportunities for language learners to engage in direct communication with speakers of the language being studied, hence projects were set up to provide such occasions for what was seen as more 'authentic' language learning (Belz, 2002; Belz & Thorne, 2006; Furstenberg et al., 2001). This occurred very much as a bottom-up or grassroots practice of individual practitioners creating informal class-to-class partnerships and collaboratively developing shared curricula and activities for their students to engage in (Dooly, 2008; Kern et al., 2004; O'Dowd, 2006). Online tandem learning projects were set up (O'Rourke, 2007) partnering students with expert speakers of their target language in order to provide opportunities for language practice. Many platforms for finding tandem partners were created, though several were subsequently bought up by commercial enterprises. One of the most long-standing projects is the TeleTandem project established in Brazil in 2006, which has been engaging Brazilian learners of languages with speakers of different languages across Europe and the United States through video conversations (Leone, 2022; Telles & Vassalo, 2006). Early telecollaboration projects had a strong focus on language learning and saw it as providing increased opportunities for practising the language being studied (see Dooly and Vinagre 2022, for an overview of VE in Foreign Language Education). The 2000s saw what has been called 'the intercultural turn' in language education and greater attention being paid to dimensions of culture. Virtual exchange became a tool to offer opportunities not only for language learning but also for intercultural engagement and VEs were designed specifically to foster intercultural learning, such as the *Cultura* project developed at MIT (discussed in Section 3). In fact, the term 'online intercultural exchange' came to be used (O'Dowd & Lewis, 2016).

---

[4] www.soliya.net.

Outside of foreign language education, VE developed above all in the field of business studies and management (Barbosa & Ferreira-Lopes, 2023), where the soft skills of intercultural/cross-cultural communication and working in global virtual teams are highly valued. Virtual exchange is seen as offering an experiential approach to intercultural learning and the development of other so-called 'twenty-first-century skills'. Launched in 2010, the X-Culture project (Godar & van Ryssen, 2022) has become a large-scale VE involving thousands of learners from over forty countries each semester (discussed in Section 4). Other fields of study in which VE is increasingly adopted are peacebuilding, education, and STEM (O'Dowd, 2023; Stevens, 2024).

1.2 Mainstreaming Virtual Exchange

Virtual exchange has become more mainstream in the last decade, at multiple levels: the institutional, national, and supranational (O'Dowd, 2023; Rubin & Guth, 2022). Institutions and networks have started to develop specific strategies and structures to support the development and implementation of VE as a form of 'internationalisation at home'. At the institutional level, the first institutions to develop units dedicated to VE were East Carolina University in 2005, and the State University New York, with its COIL Centre which was established in 2006. Following this other universities, above all in the United States, have developed similar institutional strategies, with COIL coordinators and support staff (Rubin et al., 2022). At the national and supranational levels, dedicated funding mechanisms have been set up, which support the establishment of VE. The first large-scale national funding programme for VE was the Stevens Initiative[5] in the United States, which was launched in 2015 by the State Department to support the connection of young people in the United States and the so-called Middle East and North Africa (MENA) region through VE (Helm, 2018b). Virtual exchange was identified as a cost-effective and scalable way of promoting cross-cultural experiences and developing language and communication skills, problem-solving, empathy as well as gaining self-confidence and awareness (Himelfarb, 2014).[6] The MENA region is seen as a strategic area by the United States, in particular since 9/11, hence the focus on this area. In 2023 the geographic scope of the Stevens' Initiative was expanded, and it currently includes Latin America and Ukraine. According to their website, since 2015 over 30,000 young people at school and higher education institutions have taken part in VEs funded by the initiative.[7] Other national initiatives supporting VE have since been developed, for

---

[5] www.stevensinitiative.org/.

[6] www.stevensinitiative.org/wp-content/uploads/2023/09/virtual-exchange-one-pager.pdf.

[7] The initiative is also funded by the governments of Morocco and the United Arab Emirates and the Bezos Foundation www.stevensinitiative.org/about-us/#what-we-do.

example, in Germany the IVAC project was launched in 2020[8] and in the Netherlands' VIS Project.[9] In both cases, VE is seen as offering a more accessible form of international learning for students, and a way of promoting inter-university cooperation, thus supporting universities' internationalisation objectives.

On the supranational level, the eTwinning project which aimed to connect schools across Europe was launched in 2005. In December 2021, it had over one million teachers registered and participants from more than 226,000 schools had created over 130,000 projects together.[10] Perhaps because the focus in the European higher education area has been on student mobility (Brooks et al., 2024), little attention was paid to VE. However, in 2018 the European Commission launched a three-year pilot project entitled Erasmus+ Virtual Exchange,[11] which supported the development and implementation of VE to connect young people in Europe with those in South Mediterranean countries, one of Europe's neighbourhood areas (Helm & Velden, 2021). The aims of the project included supporting intercultural dialogue and the building of partici-pants' intercultural competences. The pilot project involved over 28,000 young people in VE projects. Significantly, the project involved almost equal numbers of participants from European and South Mediterranean countries, the majority of whom had never had an international study abroad experience (Helm & Velden, 2021). Following this pilot, VE has become a component of the European Commission's regular Erasmus activities. The emphasis is on VE as a tool for higher education institutions and youth organisations in Europe to engage with similar organisations in some of the EU's external partner regions, that is, Western Balkans, Neighbourhood East, Southern Mediterranean Countries, and Sub-Saharan Africa.[12] Intra-European exchanges are not funded, the focus within Europe remains on increasing physical mobility (European Commission, 2023).

Virtual Exchange has also spread considerably in Latin America and South Africa where networks, organisations, and institutions have been developing VE strategies (Guimarães & Finardi, 2021; Rampazzo & Cunha, 2021; Rubin & Guth, 2022; Wimpenny et al., 2022). Institutions and networks are connect-ing to one another and through VE, for example, in Latin America La Red Colombiana para la Internacionalización de la Educación Superior (RCI) (Castillo et al., 2021) and the Red Latinoamericana de COIL. They see VE

---

[8] www.daad.de/en/information-services-for-higher-education-institutions/further-information-on-daad-programmes/ivac/.

[9] https://visinhetho.nl/home/about-vis/.

[10] https://education.ec.europa.eu/news/etwinning-community-of-schools-reaches-1-million-regis tered-users.

[11] https://youth.europa.eu/erasmusvirtual_en.

[12] https://erasmus-plus.ec.europa.eu/programme-guide/part-b/key-action-1/virtual-exchanges.

as offering 'more inclusive, cost-effective methods of curricular diversification' than 'traditional' internationalisation programmes based on mobility, which involve few students and have led to student disenfranchisement (Ramírez, 2022, p. 105). The same is the case for institutions in South Africa which are expanding their networks through COIL VE (Jithoo, 2020), which is seen as offering a more equitable and reciprocal form of internationalisation (Wimpenny et al., 2022). In Asia, there are also initiatives at multiple levels with some regional and bilateral initiatives with specific countries. In 2018 the bilateral, five-year US-Japan VE Inter-University Exchange Project COIL (IUEP-COIL) was launched to support both online and physical mobility, aiming to involve 100 faculty and 10,000 students in VEs.[13] In 2021, the EU launched an initiative to introduce COIL/VE in the ASEAN region in 2021, which entailed a mapping study followed by the implementation of several rounds of VE programmes between universities in the ASEAN, including the Philippines, Brunei, Malaysia, Vietnam, Cambodia, Malaysia, Laos, Indonesia, and Thailand.[14]

Much of the recent literature has focused on the mainstreaming of VE, the technicalities and institutional infrastructure and support necessary for VE to become part of regular teaching practices (O'Dowd, 2023; Rubin & Guth, 2022), above all in the so-called global north, which is where the field has developed and grown. There has been an overarching concern with the methodologies of VE, *how* to do VE. What is sometimes lost sight of is the ultimate aim of the VE. *Why* are we engaging students in VE? There is, as Imperiale points out, 'still a dearth of research that looks at the ethics and at the epistemological and ontological dimensions of telecollaboration' (Imperiale, 2021, p. 5).

1.3 Why Virtual Exchange?

There are many levels at which we can find reasons for engaging students in VE. At an institutional level, a greater number of students can be offered international or global learning experiences, since VE is a form of 'internationalisation at home' (Beelen & Jones, 2015), more accessible than mobility. For institutions VE is also a way of strengthening international partnerships beyond research and student and staff mobility, by bringing these collaborations into the classroom through teaching partnerships that engage students in VE. For educators, it is a form of collaborative teaching which can support reflection and

---

[13] www.acenet.edu/Documents/USJP-HEES-Findings-VECOIL-FactSheet.pdf.

[14] https://digest.headfoundation.org/2022/11/25/coil-virtual-exchange-as-a-driver-for-high-performance-international-partnership-building-beyond-the-response-to-covid-19/.

expansion of their own teaching. By partnering with colleagues and classes in other institutional and sociocultural contexts they may gain new insights and perspectives on their discipline, and expose students to this diversity through dynamic, experiential learning (Dooly & O'Dowd, 2018; Rubin & Guth, 2022; Starke-Meyerring & Wilson, 2008).

Virtual exchange research has focused very much on the learning outcomes and benefits for individual students: enhancing their intercultural competence or awareness (Çiftçi & Savas, 2018; O'Dowd, 2006; O'Dowd & Lewis, 2016), as well as digital literacies (Hauck, 2019), language skills and/or disciplinary knowledge, teamwork, and so on. In terms of intercultural learning, O'Dowd and Dooly (2020) report that VEs can contribute more to learning about other cultures than textbooks or static online resources. The experiential and interactional dimension of VE has been found to bring gains in pragmatic competence (Belz & Vyatkina, 2005). It allows learners to gain insights from partners' subjective accounts of their sociocultural environments and become more aware of the relativity of their own beliefs as values. Virtual exchange is also seen as facilitating the (individual's) understanding of cultures and identities as complex, changing and fluid (Helm, 2018a), as will be discussed in Section 2.

It is also important to look beyond the development of individuals' competences and take into consideration the broader educational (and societal) potential that VE has. It can of course become part of the academic industrial complex and support the kind of neoliberal internationalisation described by Marginson (2022), reinforcing coloniality and unequal relations of power. But it could also be used to challenge these dominant Eurocentric models of education and internationalisation of higher education. Building reciprocal translocal connections through VE based on relational and mutual learning can interrupt the one-way transmission of knowledge that universities in the global north and edtech companies are consolidating. Virtual exchange has the potential to expand the pluriverse, bringing the south to the north (as the north is already very much in the south) (Bagga-Gupta, 2023; Souza, 2019) by building connections among individuals and communities, helping students understand the situatedness of their knowledge. However, there is still a long way to go. The practice of VE is, no doubt, spreading geographically, adopting diverse formats, and reaching new disciplinary fields. However, international collaboration through VE, and even more so researching VE and co-authoring, is still very limited and involves few countries which are above all in the global north, as Barbosa and Ferreira-Lopes (2023) report in their recent bibliometric study of emerging trends in VE.

1.4 Typologies and Models of Virtual Exchange

Several typologies of VE have been developed based on different aspects of the exchanges. In language education a common distinction has been based on language configurations (Helm, 2015; O'Dowd, 2007), with 'bilingual' and 'bicultural' models of VE such as eTandem and *Cultura*, and 'lingua franca' VEs where a single shared language (often English) is used. The Stevens Initiative in the United States developed a 'typology of VE' (Stevens Initiative, 2021) with twelve different components to describe key aspects of VEs, including administration, type of partnership, content, activity type, duration, and technologies used. The types of partnerships may involve higher education institutions or primary or secondary institutions, informal organisations or also NGOs. The activities listed include paired courses with group project/s, asynchronous learning and international communication modules, and collaborative project-based learning. The aim of the typology was to develop a shared understanding of key concepts in VE, the different types of VE that exist and how they are developed. The intent was also to establish more consistency in the terminology used to describe VEs and to facilitate a mapping of the field of VE, which the Stevens Initiative does annually through a survey.[15]

In this Element, I make a distinction between three approaches to VE based on the framing of culture and intercultural communication and the nature of participants' interaction. I briefly describe these here without going into detail as they will be analysed in greater depth in Sections 3, 4, and 5.

Comparative approaches generally have students in partner classes engaging in activities or tasks that entail making cultural comparisons, for example, comparing cultural products such as films and/or books, comparing business cultures, education or healthcare systems, and commemoration of historical events. This approach to VE offers the potential for exploring the cultural construction of borders and differences, complex historical relations and /or dynamics of power. At the same time there are risks of methodological nationalism, reinforcing cultural stereotypes, and essentialising cultures. This will be explored further in Section 3.

Challenge-based approaches organise students from different classes into transnational virtual teams and task them with finding solutions to societal or business challenges. Students thus work in 'global virtual teams', and the different geographic location of participants is seen to bring 'cultural diversity' which is celebrated as fostering creativity and innovation in the team. At the same time (often essentialised) cultural differences can be seen as

---

[15] www.stevensinitiative.org/resources/.

presenting potential obstacles, preventing teams from finding 'solutions'. This approach will be explored further in Section 4.

Dialogue-based approaches bring together students from highly diverse contexts and engage them in sustained and facilitated dialogue addressing complex divisive issues such as conflict situations, migration, and religion. The focus here is on the dialogue process, sharing experience, and listening rather than on finding solutions to problems. Such dialogue-based exchanges offer rich opportunities for the participant (re)positioning in terms of identity and for reducing prejudice and the dehumanisation of the *other*. Yet challenges include power dynamics due to different levels of proficiency in language and connectivity. This is further explored in Section 5.

I illustrate these three approaches through the presentation of *models*, that is, seminal, large-scale VEs, and smaller-scale examples, reporting also on research findings. However, this is *my* way of putting order and trying to make sense of the different approaches to interculturality I have come across in my practice and research on VE. I believe it is useful to make these distinctions as we often find general statements in project descriptions and in the research on VE about its contribution to intercultural learning, yet what this means is not always clear. I am aware that the three approaches I present are not mutually exclusive, many VEs adopt elements of more than one. I also acknowledge that there may be other ways of framing and organising intercultural communication in VE. Finally, I would like to clarify that the aim is not to prescribe how VE should be done or to provide guidelines, but rather to use the models and examples to reflect on how interculturality is and can be approached through VE, and the impact this might have on learning.

2 Exploring Interculturality in Virtual Exchange

In the previous section, we have seen VE conceptualised as a *context* designed for intercultural communication and also a 'powerful pedagogical *strategy*' (Barbosa & Ferreira-Lopes, 2023), which allows students to develop intercultural/global competence/awareness/understanding. We find many such claims for this in discourses of VE, for example:

> virtual exchange is the perfect answer to developing intercultural competencies among students at home. While it is not a substitute for studying abroad, virtual exchange gives a taste for and is a real experience in engaging with someone from another country. (Brenda Garcia Portillo | Director of Internationalization at Home Projects – Stevens' Report)[16]

---

[16] www.stevensinitiative.org/wp-content/uploads/2022/11/2022-Survey-of-the-Virtual-Exchange-Field-Report.pdf.

It is often assumed that intercultural learning will be an *automatic* outcome of bringing students from diverse contexts to interact with one another online, in a similar vein to the belief that study abroad will lead to intercultural learning, but as research has shown, this is not always the case. Students can come back from study abroad with reinforced stereotypes (Beaven & Borghetti, 2016; Jackson, 2018) and international students at many universities experience racism and prejudice (Stein & de Andreotti, 2016). In the case of VE, scholars have reported 'failed communication', student frustration and abandonment of exchange, and 'missed' opportunities for meaningful intercultural learning (O'Dowd & Ritter, 2006; Ware, 2005).

But what exactly is meant by intercultural communication and learning? The notion of 'intercultural' was under conceptualised in the early VE literature (Lamy & Goodfellow, 2010) and there has been growing recognition that we need to critically re-assess and better understand the situatedness of this activity (Imperiale, 2021). As educators, we need to engage with 'the complex global and local relations of interwoven practices, policies, and ideologies involving, among other factors, distance, historicity, power and control as well as inequalities generated by hierarchical ordering and classification'(Train, 2012, p. 144). This is relevant to VE because it is a practice that links the local to the global and seeks to build relations among students who come from diverse contexts. Though VE has been heralded as a practice/pedagogy that can reduce power differentials and increase access to intercultural learning opportunities (Godwin-Jones, 2019), it can also reproduce and reinforce dominant knowledges, discourses, and ideologies (Wimpenny et al., 2022).

In its relatively recent history, the term intercultural communication has acquired a range of meanings and practices in the global north as it has become relevant in different fields, from the military and diplomacy (Hall, 1990; Leeds-Hurwitz, 2010) to international business (Hofstede, 2001; Meyer, 2014), foreign language education (Baker, 2022; Byram, 1997, 2008), study abroad (Beaven & Borghetti, 2016; Jackson, 2018), tourism (Jack et al., 2020), healthcare (Martin & Crichton, 2020), and so on. It has also become a field of research, within which there are diverse approaches and schools of thought (Guilherme & Souza, 2019; Hua, 2015; Piller, 2017).

This section explores the concepts of culture and cultural difference within intercultural communication, tracing their historical and theoretical foundations. It examines the emergence of culture in nineteenth-century anthropology, influenced by colonialism and the development of modern nation-states, which categorised cultures on a developmental scale to justify colonialism. The section discusses the lasting impact of colonial hierarchies and racial power dynamics, where Western knowledge is often privileged over non-Western perspectives. It critiques the dominant view of culture as a fixed entity, such as in Hofstede's cultural dimensions, advocating instead for a 'process' approach that sees culture as dynamic and evolving through interactions. Additionally, it looks at the notion of intercultural competence and the need for critical approaches that incorporate decolonial perspectives, aiming to provide an introduction to the complexities of culture and cultural difference in the broad field of intercultural communication studies. Finally, it presents the interdiscursive approach adopted in this Element and aspects of the online contexts of VE that need to be considered in developing and analysing VE.

2.1 Culture and Cultural Difference

The intercultural communication literature inevitably makes reference to notions of culture and cultural difference which, in the English language emerged with the development of the field of anthropology in the context of nineteenth-century colonialism and the development of modern nation-states (Guilherme & Souza, 2019; Piller, 2017; Sorrells, 2020). Here, culture was understood as 'a particular way of life, whether of a people, a period, a group, or humanity in general' (Williams, 1985, p. 90). One of the underlying assumptions of early anthropology was that cultures formed a cline and were positioned differently according to their development from 'savage tribes' to 'civilisation'. The hierarchy of cultures, or 'colonial difference' (Mignolo, 2002), provided the moral justification for colonialism and its so-called 'civilising mission' and became widespread not only in academic literature but in popular discourses, having spread through cultural displays in shows and exhibitions, literature, advertising, and education (Piller, 2017; Souza, 2019).

Though some scholars might suggest that this notion of a hierarchy of cultures has been overcome, decolonial and antiracist scholars point out that it still very much exists in the form of social stratification which is built from a colonial matrix of racial power, with a hierarchy where white and 'whitened' people are at the top and Indigenous peoples and Afro-descendants are at the bottom (Walsh, 2018). The colonial difference is now encoded as 'race' and supports domination and exploitation of the *other* (Souza & Duboc, 2021). This hierarchisation of people and cultures extends also to forms of knowledge. While Western/ European ways of knowing are deemed universally relevant, 'other' (i.e. gendered, racialised, indigenous . . .) ways of knowing are invisibilised or marginalised (Bagga-Gupta, 2023; Santos, 2014; Souza, 2019). This historic and colonial hierarchisation of cultures and knowledges is often overlooked in the intercultural communication literature. Rather, the focus has been on attempting to define cultures and identifying measurable characteristics that distinguish one culture from another, better known as cross-cultural research. Another key concern of intercultural research has been on developing individuals' intercultural competences/understanding/awareness. Both of these will be briefly outlined further.

2.2 Culture as Product versus Culture as Process

A prevailing and enduring view of culture in the intercultural communication literature is that of culture as a 'product' or 'entity' that can be clearly defined and distinguished from other unique 'cultures' (Baker, 2022; Piller, 2017). In this view, there are cultural products such as food, music, art, and dress but also less tangible components of culture such as beliefs, values, and behaviours. This view of culture was first described through the metaphor of an iceberg by Edward Hall (1990), in which the invisible aspects of culture are hidden under the water. Many scholars have sought to identify these dimensions of culture and have developed tools and scales for measuring and classifying cultures – which are usually defined in terms of nations – and how they compare to one another (Inglehart, 2003; Trompenaars & Hampden-Turner, 1997; Yoo et al., 2011). Geert Hofstede (Hofstede, 2001) is the best-known and most cited scholar who developed a theory of cultural dimensions in order to provide a framework for understanding how cultures differ in their values and behaviours. These dimensions include, for example, power distance, uncertainty avoidance, and individualism vs. collectivism and are measured on a scale. In Hofstede's model, culture is measured at the level of the nation-state. Many similar instruments have been developed to measure cultural values in a similar psychometric format, with over one hundred such instruments counted (Taras et al., 2009, 2023). The purpose of these frameworks and 'measurable' components is to provide guidelines when communicating with people from each culture and help decode the behaviours of the *other*. This view of culture as an entity, as something that people have or that people belong to, and associated with the nation-state is commonly found in the fields of business and foreign language education. However, it has been criticised by scholars for erasing the variation within both national and cultural boundaries (Baker, 2022; Piller, 2017; Sorrells, 2020). It is seen as essentialist, that is, reducing culture to a set of defined and unchanging characteristics that join certain groups of people and distinguish them from others. Furthermore, it ignores the 'ethnic, racial, religious, class, and/or organisational influences shaping the participants and the environments they will enter in the global context [which] are likely as salient as national cultural characteristics' (Sorrells, 2020, p. 381).

In contrast to views of culture as a clearly delineated entity with specific characteristics we can find 'process' approaches to culture (Piller, 2017) which focus on understanding culture as something that people *do*. Here it is a dynamic and evolving phenomenon that is continuously constructed, negotiated, and transformed through interactions, experiences, and contexts. In this view, culture is seen not as a set of predefined traits or characteristics but rather as complex and multifaceted. A generative construct in theorising culture as a process is *identity*. Post-structuralist views of identity, which see the establishment of identity as a social phenomenon, do not use predefined social categories such as nationality, ethnicity, or gender, but rather see identity as fluid and emergent, constructed intersubjectively through interaction (Block, 2007; Darvin & Norton, 2015). Identity is thus performed and negotiated, influenced by both individual agency and external factors (Darvin, 2016; Darvin & Sun, 2024). People engage in identity negotiation as they navigate different contexts and both individuals and groups exercise agency in constructing and contesting cultural meanings. Power dynamics, including issues of privilege and marginalisation, play a role in these processes as the meanings and experiences of dominant group members are normalised and tend to prevail over those of marginalised groups (Sorrells, 2020).

As we have seen, there is a tension between 'product' and 'process' oriented approaches to culture, between essentialism and non-essentialism. Holliday (1999, 2020) addresses this tension by focusing on 'small culture formation on the go' as the core domain of the intercultural. By small cultures (Holliday, 1999) he means the range of social groupings we form, for example, at work through friendships or interest groups, in our local communities and neighbourhoods. These small cultures are located between the two 'blocks' of 'National and other structures' and 'Cultural artefacts and products', in recognition of the fact that they are in dialogue with the essentialist grand narratives that we have been socialised into, but they are not determined by them (Holliday, 2020). It has been suggested that VEs can be seen as creating fluid and negotiated small cultures (Godwin-Jones, 2019), as students come together in a shared environment, with a common purpose and may gradually acquire shared routines, language and experiences.

2.3 Intercultural Communication

Just as there are varied definitions of culture, there are also many definitions of intercultural communication (IC), found in a wide range of disciplines. Often the term intercultural communication is used to refer to *any* form of interaction between people of different cultural backgrounds, whatever the aim or context. Baker, for example, writes that 'for many of us intercultural communication is ubiquitous' (2022, p. 20) due to globalisation, the large movements of people across geographic and cultural borders as well as the greater connectivity offered to us through digital communications. For others, intercultural communication is not mere contact, but rather the aim of the interaction, the idea of mediating and negotiating with attention to cultural framings. In the Cambridge Introduction to Intercultural Communication, for example, Rings and Rasinger (2022) define intercultural communication as follows:

> mediation aimed at creating mutual understanding between individuals or groups of different cultural backgrounds. That mediation includes exchange and negotiation of common ground and differences with particular focus on the cultural frames that shape interpretations of verbal and non-verbal behaviour as well as the results of that behaviour, e.g. particular norms, beliefs, products, systems and institutions. (Rings & Rasinger, 2022, p. 22)

Several scholars have adopted an 'interdiscursive approach' (Baker 2022; Holliday, 2011; Hua 2018; Piller, 2017) drawing on the work of Scollon and Scollon who 'ask instead how and under what circumstances concepts such as culture are produced by participants as relevant categories . . . who has introduced cultural as a relevant category, for what purposes and with what consequences?' (Scollon & Scollon, 2001, pp. 544–545). This is the approach I adopt in this Element as the aim is not to provide guidelines on how educators should go about implementing VE but rather to encourage reflection on how intercultural communication is (perhaps implicitly) conceptualised in VE projects.

2.3.1 Intercultural/Global Competence/Citizenship

Much of the intercultural communication research has been geared to defining and understanding how to communicate 'effectively' in intercultural situations – though of course effectiveness depends very much on the aims of the communication and who defines effectiveness. Over the last few decades, and across different fields, a range of frameworks have emerged to define intercultural competence (Bennett, 2015; Byram, 1997; Deardorff, 2009) but it is beyond the scope of this Element to provide an exhaustive summary. In the European context, a key reference point for many educators in foreign language education and VE has been Byram's model of Intercultural Communicative Competence (1997). This model describes the knowledge, skills, and attitudes necessary to be an 'intercultural speaker', that is, somebody who can effectively navigate and mediate between different cultural contexts. It was developed as an educational model, with elements to equip language learners to engage in intercultural communication in the language they are studying and has been widely referenced in the VE literature, though like many early frameworks for intercultural competence, it was developed for interactions in physical spaces and study abroad. More recently, the term 'global competence' has gained popularity in educational contexts as the OECD has developed a framework for teaching and testing this construct (OECD, 2018). Global competence, according to the OECD, refers to the capacity to analyse global and intercultural issues critically, to understand and appreciate the perspectives and worldviews of others, to engage in open, appropriate, and effective interactions with people from different cultures, and to act for collective well-being and sustainable development. This framework has three dimensions, the cognitive, affective, and behavioural.

In the context of European foreign language education, Byram expanded his model of intercultural communicative competence to incorporate citizenship education, further developing the political component of acting interculturally (Byram, 2008; Porto et al., 2018). He classifies different levels of political engagement, starting with the 'pre-political' level, which entails engagement with others and reflecting critically on their own assumptions and those of others. The 'political' level involves taking actions to generate change – in their own societies or, at a higher level, as a transnational group. Global citizenship frameworks have gained ground in recent years (Akkari & Maleq, 2020; Andreotti & Souza, 2014; Bourne, 2020), also in the field of VE (Benini et al., 2022; Helm et al., 2023; O'Dowd, 2020). These citizenship frameworks are seen to stand in contrast with competence frameworks, which have been critiqued for prioritising the actions and achievements of the individual to make them more competitive in the global economy (Joris et al., 2022). However, there are contrasting discourses around global citizenship. On the one hand we find the relevance of values, social responsibility, and active citizenry, while on the other there remains the neoliberal discourse that focuses on the competitive global individual citizen, with a homogenising universalist epistemology (Andreotti & Souza, 2014; Guimarães & Finardi, 2021; Pais & Costa, 2020). Andreotti and Souza (2014) point out that often global citizenship initiatives ignore the 'complex historical, cultural and political nature of the issues, identities and perspectives embedded in global/local processes and events' (p. 1) and reinforce simplistic us/them, here/there binaries that postcolonial scholars have denounced.

2.3.2 Critical Intercultural Communication Studies

Critical intercultural communication scholars argue that much of the literature on intercultural communication relies on neat classifications of cultural difference and unquestioned definitions of otherness whilst some of the most complex and contested challenges of today's multicultural societies are avoided. Ferri (2018), for example, argues for an ethical approach to intercultural communication that engages 'in the debates that are most poignant in the current climate of hostility towards "the other": refugees and asylum seekers, ethnic minorities, immigrants, women, the disabled, and LGBTQI'. (2018, p. 6). Writing from a philosophical background, she focuses on the 'inter-' in intercultural communication and the ethical relation with the other. She problematises the tendency in intercultural communication research and training to 'fix meaning under the pre-established script of communicative competence and the effective transmission of content' (2018, p. 67). Furthermore, she critiques the discourse of effectiveness and 'the ideal of a competent intercultural speaker endowed with the characteristics of tolerance, flexibility, reflexivity, ability to decenter and open mindedness [which] hides the material conditions in which the individual is embedded' (p. 82). As Imperiale (2021) points out, the majority of models for intercultural communication were developed in Western contexts at times of peace where 'mobility is taken for granted as a prerequisite and as an objective of ICC' (p. 23). The question she raises is what happens to our frameworks when mobility is taken away? In her view, intercultural communication education should foreground context, which comprises the freedoms individuals have, and the relational dimension of intercultural communication.

Scholars working from a decolonial standpoint highlight the issue of power and epistemologies, which cannot be ignored when discussing interculturality and educational exchange. Concepts such as the coloniality of power and of knowledge make visible the hierarchies of knowledge whereby Western/ northern knowledge is valued and seen to be universally valid and relevant (Mignolo, 2012; Quijano, 2000; Souza, 2019; Walsh, 2018). *Other* forms of (Indigenous, racialised, feminist, and subaltern) knowledge are invisibilised, or at best marked as 'local' (Souza, 2019). Intercultural communication from this perspective thus implies expanding the ecology of knowledges and making 'pluriversal knowledge', bringing the south to the north (Bagga-Gupta, 2023). Souza (2022) warns us, however, that it is not merely an epistemological issue of expanding the ecology of knowledges by bringing a greater diversity of knowledges to the table. He argues for a move from the 'what' to the 'who', suggesting that we should be looking at who owns the table, who does the inviting to the table and who is considered eligible to be invited. This calls on us to reflect also on the question of funding of VE (when VE is funded, as this is not always the case) as this can have an impact on the partnerships established. Some major funders of VE, such as the U.S. State Department's Stevens Initiative and the European Commission, decide which countries or regions VE partners should be located in for their programmes. On an institutional level, some universities prioritise certain partnerships by providing funding or incentives for exchanges with these partners, but not for others. These choices are influenced by political motivations and interests, as VE, like study abroad and scholarships, is used as a tool of soft power (Himelfarb, 2014).

2.4 Researching Intercultural Communication

In her critical introduction to intercultural communication, drawing on the work of Scollon and Scollon, the sociolinguist Ingrid Piller (2017) distinguishes between three approaches to the study of intercultural communication. *Cross-cultural communication* studies start from the assumption that distinct cultural groups exist and explore cultures and communicative practices comparatively. Within this paradigm, communication systems of the groups are here considered independently of any social interaction (Scollon and Scollon, 2001). Studies in *intercultural communication* also start from an assumption of difference, but here cultures are explored in interaction with each other rather than comparatively. This approach is often adopted in VE studies, where the behaviour of different student groups in their interactions, or their reactions to an exchange are explored. The third approach is the *interdiscursive approach*. Here there is no a priori notion of cultural identity, rather the focus is on how culture is made relevant in interaction or text (Scollon & Scollon, 2001).

In this Element, I take on this latter approach by exploring how culture is made relevant in the pedagogic design of VEs through analysis of texts *about* VE. These texts are important as they serve to create the situated context of a VE. We could say that in setting up a VE for intercultural communication, educators are 'doing culture' and intercultural communication, as they are making culture relevant. They conceptualise intercultural communication for their students and define what 'lines of difference' they see as relevant for the exchange – these lines may be geographic/national, regional, linguistic, disciplinary, religious, ethnic, political, professional, and so on. The educators' framing of the exchange might position the student-participants as members/ representatives of a particular nation or region, for example, and/or as experts of a specific discipline or future professionals (Helm & Hauck, 2022). This does not mean that the students will necessarily align themselves with these positionings, or limit themselves to these, for participants have agency that they will use in their interactions to position themselves and each other (Helm, 2018a). Furthermore, these positionings are in constant flux, they do not remain fixed throughout an interaction, they are negotiated. The questions I ask as I explore models of VE in this Element are adapted from those asked by Scollon & Scollon (2001, p. 544–545):

• How is culture made relevant in the pedagogical design/context of a VE?
• What impact might this have on student positioning within the exchange and on intercultural learning?
• What are the opportunities for learning in this approach to culture and intercultural communication, and what are the limitations or risks?

In researching intercultural communication from an interdiscursive approach, analysis of the context of communication is important, since shared knowledge of the context is the basis on which participants interpret the meaning of speech events (Scollon & Scollon, 2001). Much of the early literature on intercultural communication has been written about interactions that take place in physical contexts – be it classrooms, offices, shops, tourist environments, universities, and so on. As we grow up, we acquire experience and understanding of these types of contexts and are socialised into the discourse practices of these spaces. Online worlds as contexts for intercultural communication are now also being explored (Jones & Hafner, 2021; Macfadyen et al., 2004; Schroder et al., 2023). Whilst students are likely to have experience of communication and socialisation in a range of online contexts and discourse communities, VE is quite different and 'unknown', since it is not (yet) an institutionalised educational practice or recognisable academic genre like a lecture, seminar, or debate. Students will often enter a VE only with information about the context provided by the developers of the exchange and their teachers, and on this basis will create expectations.

The fact that VEs do not take place in a physical space, or a specific institution or even geographic territory does not mean that they take place on 'neutral ground'. The online environment and communication tools used for the exchange 'are produced by and productive of culturally organised systems of activity' (Thorne, 2016, p. 189). The many available forms of digital communication differ semiotically from one another and from offline communications and have an impact on the interactions that take place (Kern, 2014; Kramsch & Thorne, 2002). For example, whilst asynchronous text-based communication allows time for reflection before writing, synchronous communication is more immediate, but means that turns must be short and frequent. Text-based communication allows for a degree of anonymity, with the advantages and challenges this presents, whilst video-based allows for more online presence. Furthermore, the ways we use online communication tools are learned through the communities we are socialised into. The 'cultures-of-use' framework acknowledges that:

> like all human creations, communication tools are cultural tools that carry interactional and relational associations, preferred uses (and correspondingly dispreferred uses), and expectations of genre- and register-specific communicative activity, all of which are learned through processes of language and tool socialisation via participation in particular online speech communities. (Thorne, 2016, p. 185)

In VE this adds a layer of complexity to intercultural communication, 'an additional axis of potential intercultural alignment and divergence' (Thorne, 2016, p. 187). That is, the communication tools chosen and the ways they are used may differ amongst participants in a VE, and this may cause tensions.

2.5 Analysing Virtual Exchange as a Context of Intercultural Communication

Studying VE as a context of intercultural communication entails looking at much more than the online space and modes/tools of communication. As I said earlier in this section, a VE is constructed discursively and pedagogically, with specific objectives in mind. The designers of a VE set up interactions amongst participants, design activities for them to engage in and in so doing orchestrate situated contexts for intercultural communication. It is the discursive and pedagogic set-up of a VE that initially makes culture relevant and positions participants in a certain way. As the exchange progresses, the situated context of the VE may become a 'small culture' in and of itself, co-created by the exchange participants, though of course this does not happen in a void. Any VE will be influenced by the objectives, cultures, contexts, experiences, and beliefs of the educators/designers and the participants in the exchange. There will also be factors that have an impact on the power dynamics of the exchange, which begin from the design phase. In analysing the situated context of a VE, it can be useful to consider several components.

Setting

This regards the history and set up of the VE, starting from the macro-level of funding (if relevant), to the partnership – that is, the institutions or organisations involved in both the design and implementation of the VE; the socio-political and material realities of the partners involved (Jimenez et al., 2022); the historical and geo-political relations between the nations/regions of the partners involved; the discoursal construction of the VE as found on the website or partners' description of the exchange.

Partnership, Participants, and Configuration

Who and how many are the partners of the VE? Who are the participants in the interaction? Just students or also facilitators or teachers? How are the participants presented, and what are their roles? How are they positioned? As members from a class from a specific nation, specialists in a specific discipline, future professionals? How are students configured for interaction? Does communication take place in dyads/triads/groups?

Purpose

What are the main (stated) purposes for communication in the VE?

There may be different purposes for communication in different phases of an exchange, and of course individuals may have their own purposes and objectives for communicating in an exchange – which may differ from those of their partners and of the VE designers:

- Exchanging information in order to acquire knowledge about (aspects of) the different cultural contexts (e.g. education systems, recruitment processes, history, literature . . .).
- Collaborating in order to complete tasks, develop a product (e.g. website, presentation, architectural design, theatre piece . . .), or find a solution to a problem or challenge.
- Gaining exposure to different perspectives and understandings of social, political, historical, environmental, or other issues.
- Practising a foreign language and/or developing communicative competence.
- Building relationships, translocal solidarities, and networks of individuals.

In relation to purpose, it can be useful to make a distinction between communication where there is a need to *converge*, that is, to come to an agreement in order to solve a problem, complete a task or project, and *divergent* communication where differences (of opinion, experiences, values . . .) can be explored and valorised. In the former, there is often a focus on finding common ground and suppressing differences in order to come to an agreement, whilst in the latter convergence is not necessary. This can open up space for exploration and engagement with diverse knowledges, experiences, and opinions.

Topic

What are the main topics of the VE? Who decides these? Is the VE focussed only on the disciplinary field(s) of the participating students or more general? Is the exchange transdisciplinary, creatively involving partners of different disciplinary areas? Are the topics of local and/or global relevance? Are certain topics intentionally avoided? Why?

Modes of Communication

What tools and platforms are used for the VE? Who chooses these? What impact does this have on communication? As mentioned earlier, the mediating artefacts of online intercultural communication are more than neutral tools, to the extent that they can be considered participants in the interaction (Thorne, 2016). Much of the early research on VE regarded above all text-based communication which, until the Covid-19 pandemic, was the dominant mode in many VEs, with researchers looking at the affordances of asynchronous and synchronous text-based tools (Avgousti, 2018; Chun, 2011; Çiftçi & Savaş, 2018; Godwin-Jones, 2019). Since the pandemic, video-mediated communication has become ingrained in many people's everyday lives. The many semiotic resources and modes that are co-present make video communication a rich and often more complex environment than offline communication events (Sindoni, 2023). There are also important issues of access to platforms and connectivity, which may be uneven amongst partners and, in relation to coloniality, ownership of platforms and student data (Couldry & Mejias, 2023).

Language

What language(s) are used for the exchange? What are the implications of this? Online intercultural communication is mediated not only through tools but also through language, which can have an impact on interactions and dimensions of power, particularly if we consider that identity is in a large part mediated by language proficiency (Piller, 2017). In foreign language education VEs have traditionally been bilingual', involving the 'target languages' of the participants involved (Helm, 2015). In other disciplinary areas most VEs take place in a 'lingua franca', usually English, which has become the principle medium of intercultural communication (Jackson, 2020). It is not the English language in and of itself that is problematic, but rather the monolingual, monocultural mindset, and ideologies such as native speakerism and hierarchisation of varieties of English that may accompany the use of English and serve to reinforce coloniality and unequal power dynamics (Souza, 2019).

In the following sections of this Element, I outline three approaches to culture and intercultural communication in VE. For each section, I have selected specific cases of VEs which I outline briefly in terms of the context, drawing on the elements described earlier. Subsequently, I discuss the opportunities for intercultural learning as well as limitations and risks, for which I draw on some of the research findings related to the cases described, including in some cases my own research.

3 Comparative Approaches

Comparative approaches are used in both research and teaching in a range of academic disciplines, such as literature, anthropology, politics, law, sociology, and religion (Adams, 2021). As a method of analysis, a comparative approach involves examining and evaluating similarities and differences between two or more entities, systems, processes, concepts, or any other elements and is often carried out on an international or cross-national level (Hantrais, 2008). It is often used to gain a deeper understanding of the subject matter and can lead to greater awareness of the underlying assumptions of one's own conceptual framework because it requires scholars to make these assumptions explicit, question how and why frameworks develop and consider what might count as similarities and differences (Adams, 2021; Hoecke, 2021). Comparative approaches are common in language, culture, and intercultural communication studies, as briefly discussed in Section 2, where they are often described as *cross*-cultural communication studies.

One of the most common approaches to VE involves educators working in two different national/socio-institutional contexts collaborating in the development of a joint curriculum and sets of activities. This approach characterises COIL VE (Rubin & Guth, 2022) and the telecollaborative model (O'Dowd, 2006, 2023). It has been and continues to be widely used in foreign language VE and other disciplinary areas such as education, history, politics, and healthcare, as will be discussed in this section. This approach to VE could be said to combine a cross-cultural with an intercultural approach since it often entails comparisons of cultural products, practices and/or processes, while at the same time engaging students from diverse sociocultural contexts in some form of interaction. In this section, I first illustrate the *Cultura* model, which has been widely adopted in foreign language education (Chun, 2014). I then explore comparative approaches to intercultural learning in VEs in the fields of teacher education, history, and political sciences. Some of the research findings about these and other VEs that adopt a comparative approach will be presented in the discussion of the opportunities and limitations or risks of this approach (in Sections 3.4 and 3.5).

3.1 The *Cultura* Project

A pioneering VE adopting a comparative approach is the *Cultura* Project,[17] developed in the field of foreign language education in the late 1990s at MIT (Furstenberg et al., 2001) and still running today. *Cultura* was designed as a 'concrete methodology for learning about another culture', which could be adapted for different languages and cultures and be taken to different layers of depth. Indeed, on the website exchanges have been carried out also in Russian, Spanish, and German. It has become a 'model' for VE, providing inspiration for many subsequent exchanges (Chun, 2014, 2015; Furstenberg & English, 2016; García & Crapotta, 2007). *Cultura* is summarised as follows on the project website:

> *Cultura* offers a cross-cultural approach which has students observe, compare and analyze similar materials from their respective cultures, make observations and draw preliminary hypotheses, then exchange viewpoints with each other, via on-line discussion forums. Working with a large array of materials, they test their initial hypotheses and gradually reach a deeper understanding of the nature and origin of the differences they have observed.[18]

Though national culture is not explicitly mentioned, the classes in the exchange are located in different countries, the materials used are drawn from national contexts (the United States and France in the original *Cultura* project) and are in the national languages of these countries. The framing of the project thus brings to the fore nation and language as the boundaries of culture. The dimensions of culture to be explored are, according to the project developers, what Edward Hall (1990) defined as 'the silent language', or the hidden dimension – that is, 'the values, attitudes, beliefs, and concepts inherent in another culture; to understand how people interact, look at the world and frame their thoughts and ideas'. National/cultural/linguistic differences are made salient to the participants through the activity of comparison – starting from the comparison of questionnaire responses generated by students to the comparison of other types of data, which will be discussed further. Comparing and contrasting similar documents from two cultures through the process of juxtaposition makes it possible to see differences and similarities that would not otherwise be visible (Furstenberg et al., 2001). It allows students to start 'seeing', for instance, the different values given to words, the negative or positive connotations, and the various attitudes toward events or situations. This constitutes the first step toward deciphering and understanding what these differences may reveal and signify. The first materials that students compare are their responses to online

---

[17] https://cultura.mit.edu/.   [18] https://cultura.mit.edu/what-is-cultura paragraph 4 Approach.

forms that have been designed to elicit attitudes towards certain behaviours and cultural 'rich points' (Agar, 1994), that is, responses that might be puzzling and differ from the students' usual frame of reference and will require a translation between the cultures and languages of the groups. The surveys consist of:

- 'Word Associations' (e.g. Individualism / *Individualisme*, Freedom / *Liberté*, Police / *Police*);
- Sentence completion (e.g. A rude person is someone who . . . / *Une personne impolie est quelqu'un qui ...*); and
- Situation reaction (e.g. A police officer stops you in the street and asks for your ID. / *Un agent de police vous arrête dans la rue et vous demande vos papiers.*).

Student responses to the surveys are anonymised and made publicly visible on the project website for the classes (and the broader general public) to see.[19]

Participants in the exchange are implicitly positioned as anthropologists/ curious explorers of the 'other' (national) language and culture as they are tasked with analysing and making hypotheses about the patterns and meanings they find in their peers' responses to the questionnaires. They are also positioned as cultural informants, who can confirm or disconfirm/disprove their international peers' 'hypotheses' about 'their culture'. In their interactions, they are supposed to ask questions and provide explanations about their survey responses and analyses, how and why they relate to their respective cultures. Below is a post from a student[20] on the forum about the word 'individualism/*individualisme*', a word which often generates quite different responses from groups, with students in France generally giving negative connotations, in particular selfishness and solitude, whilst students in the United States generally associate it with more positive words such as freedom and expression.

> Additionally, as Americans (not all of us, but speaking from my perspective) we were taught to embrace our differences and to feel comfortable with who we are. I believe that because of this I associate these words such as 'freedom' and 'identity.' This leads me to wonder what xxx asked – are the French students simply more educated in philosophy than the MIT students and therefore hold this view? Or, alternatively, is the French culture more conforming and encouraging of uniformity which leads to these opinions on individualism? How do we define individualism and uniqueness differently?[21]

---

[19] https://cultura.mit.edu/cultura-exchanges-archive.

[20] Student responses are published on the exchange website and available for others to analyse and explore.

[21] https://cultura.mit.edu/cultura-exchanges/year/2020/semester/spring/host/mit/guest/enseirb.

We see how she positions herself as 'American', and acknowledges that not all classmates are American, or perhaps that not all classmates share her view on being taught to embrace differences, as she reflects on how her education may have shaped her responses. She then poses her hypotheses and questions to her French peers. It is difficult to sense the tone of the post since it could be interpreted as demonstrating humility or sarcasm with the comment 'simply more educated' and a negative evaluation of French culture as 'conforming' and 'encouraging of uniformity'. The role of the educators working with their classes here would be in helping students dig deeper and reflect on their interpretations of their peers' responses and their own cultural assumptions.

The surveys are just the first step in the process, which is framed as a journey, as students are then led to further explore the 'target culture' in modules that explore different kinds of cultural products or resources, such as newspapers, statistical datasets (e.g. from the US Census Bureau and INSEE (Institut National de la Statistique et des Etudes Economiques), and opinion polls, key documents (e.g. constitutions), remakes of films, and novels. According to the project developers, this further exploration is key to developing a deeper understanding of culture as it exposes students to a multiplicity of viewpoints and perspectives (Furstenberg & English, 2016). Accessing datasets, for example, allows students to compare their findings so far to broader sets of information such as statistics and opinion polls which will either confirm or contradict some of their earlier findings. Exploring historical/constitutional documents might allow them to understand the legacy behind historical factors which contribute to shaping values, practices, and behaviours.

It is important to point out that in the original project developed by MIT, the questionnaires are completed and interactions are carried out in the students' first/main language as this is where cultural 'rich points' can be found, such as the notions and significance attached to certain words or specific ways of using language for interaction (Furstenberg et al., 2021). The priority of the project developers was to focus precisely on the cultural meaning of language, with the teachers and their peers as mediators. Adaptations of the *Cultura* project, however, have moved away from the focus on language/culture and often cultural comparisons are carried out using a lingua franca, usually English (Chun, 2015; Furstenberg & English, 2016; García & Crapotta, 2007).

3.2 Comparative Approach in Teacher Education Virtual Exchanges

Comparative approaches to culture are widely used in teacher education, a field in which VE is increasingly adopted (Dooly & Sadler, 2013; Hauck et al., 2020).

The EVALUATE project was a large-scale EC-funded project which investigated the impact of VE on students and teachers of Initial Teacher Education between 2017 and 2019. In this project the 'progressive exchange model' was used (Baroni et al., 2019; O'Dowd & Ware, 2009) whereby participants first get to know each other by exchanging information, they then engage in cultural comparisons and finally work together on a collaborative product. Three sets of task sequences were developed to support the educators implementing the VEs.[22]

In one of the task sequences, for the second phase entailing comparison, *Cultura*-style questionnaires were used but adapted to the topic of education. Many of the sentence completion prompts provided in the Teacher's Manual make specific reference to the national contexts, for example, students were asked to complete sentences such as:

- To improve primary schools *in my country* we need to . . .
- The biggest problem is primary schools *in my country* is . . . .[23]

The guidelines for exchange coordinators specify that when the questionnaires are completed and juxtaposed, students ought to work in their local classes to look for differences and similarities in the questionnaire results. They should then discuss their findings with their partner class in their international working group forums in their VLE. Students are then called upon to interview one another, and once again prompts are provided for comparison:

- Comparing the role of religion in primary schools *in our countries.*
- How English is taught in primary schools *in our countries.*
- How ICT is used in primary schools *in our countries.*

Culture in these tasks is defined in terms of nation, and students are positioned as nationals of a specific country and 'experts' on the national education systems. The focus is on identifying similarities and differences in the national education systems and perspectives on these. Other tasks, however, make relevant local identities, and encourage participants to make links between the local and the European level. Participants' future professional identities as teachers are also made relevant in the setup of the exchange by relating activities to the teaching profession, for example, in collaborative project-based tasks which ask them to create teaching materials or activities for their future classes. In this type of collaborative activity, the 'small culture' of the transnational group as collaborating future teachers is also brought to the fore.

---

[22] www.unicollaboration.org/wp-content/uploads/2020/08/Task_sequences_EVALUATE.pdf.
[23] My italics

Symeonidis and Impedovo (2023) report on a VE for student teachers of various disciplines in order to enhance their professional awareness of themselves as 'European teachers' (Schratz, 2014) in teacher education. This VE adopted a similar approach, comparing Austrian and French teacher education systems 'to enhance student teachers' professional awareness of themselves as European teachers (Symeonidis and Impedovo, 2023, p. 822). After being introduced to the European teacher model, they were asked to compare, analyse, and critically evaluate national and international reports on the teaching profession in the two countries, and then to exchange experiences and anecdotes on teacher education in their contexts. Their final task was a group presentation on the potential benefits and challenges of becoming a European teacher. As in the Evaluate project, national and professional identities are made relevant in the framing of the project, as well as European identity. National identity is relevant to these exchanges because education systems are legislated nationally, and indeed education systems are where young people's (and future teachers') national identities are formed and nurtured (Billig, 1995; Piller, 2017). As pointed out by a participant in the study:

> [O]ur general training does not focus on Europe, or what other countries are doing, and at no time are we advised to consider that. So we are being trained to be teachers in France rather than in Europe. (ST, France) (Symeonidis & Impedovo, 2023, p. 832)

What this quote highlights is how a European or global professional teacher identity presupposes critical awareness of the strong national aspects of teaching and teacher education in a specific country.

In their VE for future teachers in Georgia in the United States and Johannesburg in South Africa on social justice education, Carolin and Johnson's (2023) starting point was that:

> There is a comparable contextual basis for the discussions between students at these universities: South Africa and Georgia have similar educational contexts where, despite de jure racial segregation being prohibited, de facto racialized school segregation continues into the present. (Carolin & Johnson, 2023, p. 1)

From this shared premise, they explored social justice education, as both epistemology and praxis. The topic of segregation and desegregation of public schools was the core of the exchange and participants explored personal experiences of education, the relevance of the past in the present in relation to race and inequality, and finally the role of social justice education. Podcasts and news articles were shared with the participants to ensure they had a common starting point. In this VE, as well as their national identities, students' racial/

ethnic identities and socioeconomic status were made relevant through the choice of topic and the foregrounding of students' identities and experiences. This is one of few VEs I have come across that explicitly addresses racism and inequality, drawing powerful historical links across space and time.

3.3 Cultural Comparisons in History and Political Science Virtual Exchanges

Comparative approaches have been adopted in VEs in the field of history, which is a disciplinary area that has great potential for exploring culture and engaging in intercultural dialogue. Many of the seeds of societal conflict are deeply rooted in diverging interpretations, understanding, and exploitation of historical events. In fact several scholars of critical intercultural communication sustain that a historical approach is essential for critical cultural awareness (Ferri, 2018; Guilherme & Souza, 2019), because meaning-making and knowledge production are located within unequal histories and relations of power.

Cioltan-Drăghiciu and Stanciu (2020) carried out a VE over three successive years looking at how specific events from the First World War were being remembered in Romania and Hungary one hundred years later. They saw this as a way to raise students' awareness 'about stereotypes and the ways the two nations had created "mutually incompatible fairy tales" (Hobsbawm, 1996) to legitimise their existence' (Cioltan-Drăghiciu & Stanciu, 2020, p. 38). In the framing of this exchange, culture is made relevant from the point of view of 'cultural remembrance', that is, how historical events are remembered by a society. It is studied from a critical point of view, with students engaging in activities such as discourse analysis of advertisements for commemorating events and art festivals. Cioltan-Drăghiciu and Stanciu (2020) wanted to highlight to students that historical events are often presented as subjective constructions that are used to manipulate people for political purposes. Amongst the quotes cited by the authors is this comment where we see how a student positions themself and points to the realisation that there are often multiple perspectives on historical events:

> The subject chosen for this project allowed me, as a Romanian history student, to see another side of the discourse regarding these events and made me realise that such controversial events cannot be analysed just from one perspective. (Cioltan-Drăghiciu & Stanciu, 2020, p. 45)

This exchange shows how intercultural communication can take place between close neighbours who happen to be on different sides of a historical event that has shaped national identity and narratives in the two contexts. Other exchanges use two or more different issues that are of historical, political, and cultural relevance to each group of students, but through the exchange they see these through the eyes of their peers whose readings of the events might be different. For example, an exchange on comparative politics between classes in the United States and Germany looked at political culture and the impact of the past in the two countries (Olsen et al., 2006). In a co-taught class, the educators provided students with academic literature on the concept of political culture and the legacies of slavery for race relations in the United States and on the 'usable past' in Germany and its role in shaping German identity and foreign policy. Each week of their nine-week exchange, groups of students posted a short summary, analysis, and reaction to the materials to asynchronous forums, and others would post their thoughts and reactions to these. The content from these written exchanges provided the starting point for classes with their professors and fast-paced synchronous chats.

King de Ramirez (2021) reports on an exchange between students in the 'Arizona-Sonora Megaregion', that is, between students living on either side of the US-Mexico border, with the aim of critically examining their perceptions of the neighbouring country and the interconnectivity between them. She says students were positioned as 'active agents' in the communities being studied and as 'investigators' supposed to seek opportunities 'to increase their knowledge of their home community and neighboring community through sharing experiences, questioning prior knowledge, and developing new perspectives' (p. 88). She found that they gained a understanding of educational systems, employment opportunities, and economy and that the exchange allowed students to challenge stereotypes and understand the personal impact of policies on people.

A project involving educators and students from political science, in this case in Germany and South Africa, aimed to address epistemic asymmetries in the field of peacebuilding, human mobility, and mediation (Khoo et al., 2020). The project is framed not as a VE, but rather a cross-site teaching project that entailed jointly developing curricula that acknowledge historical processes of privileging certain kinds of knowledge and bringing into the course a plurality of perspectives.[24] This is done first through collaboration in the selection of inputs such as readings, video materials, scientific literature, artworks, and invited speakers related to the jointly taught courses over several years, which have covered themes such as migration, mediation, and international conflict resolution. At the same time students are positioned as 'experts of their respective perspectives and disciplinary backgrounds' (Khoo et al., 2020, p. 64) and are expected to work on a cross-site basis to engage in 'joint knowledge production'

---

[24] https://cross-site-teaching.phil.hhu.de/about-us/.

through research or artistic projects. The main aim of the project, in fact, is 'to broaden both students' and lecturers' perspectives on theoretical, empirical, and methodological approaches via a joint learning process' (Khoo et al., 2020, p. 63). The words 'culture' or 'intercultural' are not mentioned on the project website or publications about the project, rather it is framed in terms of decoloniality, aiming to address intellectual imperialism (the domination of another people's way of thinking), academic dependency (conditioning the development of academic disciplines in dominated countries), and epistemic injustice (asymmetries in knowledge production and marginalisation of existing knowledge). This project explicitly seeks to decolonise the curriculum, not merely through exposure to a diversity of perspectives but also through active engagement with and reflection on theories of coloniality.

3.4 Opportunities

Virtual exchanges which employ cultural comparisons as in the *Cultura* project and engage students in interactions, whether synchronous or asynchronous, have been found to develop participants' cultural knowledge and attitudes as well as language skills (Chun, 2015; O'Dowd and Dooly, 2020). Virtual exchanges support the understanding of the polysemic nature of words, how the 'same' word may represent a completely different concept or have different connotations in different languages/cultures (Chun, 2015).

Engaging in cultural comparisons and in-depth explorations of cultural 'rich points' in the 'target' language and culture positions students as both ethnographers and informants, seeking, receiving, and providing subjective accounts of their sociocultural environments. They may be asked to explain certain structures, behaviours, events, and practices which they took for granted as being transparent and clear. This allows for a more nuanced understanding of the partiality of cultural knowledge and increased awareness of the cultural embeddedness of their own beliefs, values, and practices (O'Dowd & Dooly, 2020). What they have considered universal may become local and marked, and they may learn more about and reflect on their own positionality, as Symeonidis and Impedovo report below in relation to their project with student teachers (STs):

> Reflecting on one's own professional awareness beyond national boundaries was something that the students had neither considered nor experienced before. In this regard, 'it was interesting to experience how differently the two systems function; the differences are much greater than I thought. This allowed us to think outside what we know, beyond our own little worlds' (ST, Austria). (Symeonidis & Impedovo, 2023, p. 832)

At the same time, providing a kaleidoscope of viewpoints, expanding students' research with new sources of information complexifies culture and reduces the chances of simplistic generalisations becoming the focus of debate (Furstenberg & English, 2016). The constructivist approach adopted in *Cultura* means that the students are actively involved in gradually developing an understanding of the subject matter. Through their interactions with the materials, their peers and, importantly, their teachers, students are required to continuously re-elaborate their hypotheses not only about the 'other' culture but also themselves (Furstenberg et al., 2001). This engagement with complexity applies to lecturers as well as students, as Khoo et al. (2020) wrote about their exchange, 'the seminar thus not only turned into a journey of learning about one's own positionality and perspective for the students but moreover for all lecturers involved' (p. 67).

Focusing on specific contexts and histories offers great potential for exploring the cultural construction of borders and differences, complex historical relations, and dynamics of power. Olsen et al. (2006) found that students' knowledge of the other country's political cultures greatly increased as well as their intercultural understanding. This was held to be particularly significant because few of their students had direct experience with foreign cultures and, as educators, they struggled to make the material seem alive and relevant to students. Khoo et al.'s (2020) exchange was a response to the historical privileging of certain knowledge systems in the curricula of the universities of Pretoria and Düsseldorf. They observed that using the framework of epistemic justice in their exchange allowed them to draw attention to 'how we recognise people as knowers, how people might be wronged as knowers, and how knowers with power might knowingly or unknowingly perpetrate forms of injustice' (Khoo et al., 2020, p. 57). Students learnt to question dominant knowledge production processes and engage with the concept of epistemic diversity and justice:

> Apparently, students based in Pretoria were able to ask their German fellows in detail about recent elections, the current government and its policies. German students were struck by their sparse knowledge about South Africa in particular and Africa in general. Experiencing these asymmetries on the interpersonal level helped students to reflect on their own positionalities as both subjects and objects of the collaboration project. (Khoo et al., 2020, p. 66).

Virtual exchanges that incorporate historical and decolonial approaches may thus provide a tool to address 'the critical need for re-visiting historical narratives and experiences which continue to be based on naturalised imagined dichotomies and separations of territories, peoples, and ideas or what gets glossed as culture' (Bagga-Gupta, 2023).

3.5 Limitations and Risks

One of the inherent risks of a comparative approach is that we are further naturalising the nation-state as the unit of analysis both in the exchanges themselves and research related to these. In language education exchanges this often comes with the reinforcement of the one language one nation ideology (Lamy & Goodfellow, 2010). It is easy to fall into the trap of describing bilateral exchanges (on websites, course descriptions, and in research papers) and defining the partner classes and the students themselves by the nation-states they are located in, so we might have, for example, a collaboration between Spain and United States nursing students (Appel et al., 2023), or a Hong Kong-Germany telecollaboration (Fuchs, 2019). Furthermore, as we have seen in Sections 3.1, 3.2, and 3.3, activities entailing cultural comparisons designed for students also frequently equate culture with nation. It may seem a trivial point, but it is precisely its ubiquity and everydayness that characterises 'banal nationalism' (Billig, 1995), that is, the unnoticed, taken-for-granted signs of nationalism. Some examples Billig provides of this are the use of flags on public buildings and national maps in weather forecasts, which are signs that we also frequently find in VEs, for example, students using flags as visual representations of their national affiliation (Satar et al., 2023). In his view, it is the seemingly 'hidden' nature of banal nationalism that makes it a powerful ideology since it is rarely challenged despite being the basis for dangerous and violent nationalisms.

The use of national categories in VE positions exchange participants as members/representatives of a national culture, and they sometimes fall into the role of 'ambassadors' or even 'guardians', feeling the need to promote or defend 'their culture' (O'Dowd, 2020). What is more, engaging in cultural comparisons can risk reproducing the colonial dynamic of creating hierarchies of cultures, with students judging and evaluating the 'other' in negative terms and reinforcing a sense of 'national superiority' or 'inferiority'. Whilst it may not be possible or even desirable to entirely avoid national categories, it is important that they are addressed with a critical stance, raising awareness of issues like essentialism, prejudice, bias, racism, and the exclusion that the use of national identities can bring.

When they remain on a superficial level, comparative approaches risk accentuating a binary approach to culture, reducing the complexity and multiplicity of individuals to monolithic and essentialist national identities. Indeed, the developers of the *Cultura* exchange believe that using the questionnaires alone can be counterproductive for this precise reason and emphasise the importance of students exploring a large variety of other materials which can present a multiplicity of viewpoints, also highly contradictory ones (Furstenberg & English, 2016, p. 172). Researchers have also found that in VE interactions may emphasise what participants have in common, the 'illusion of commonality' (Helm & Baroni, 2020; Ware & Kramsch, 2005), rather than engaging with complexity. Reasons for this may be multiple, for example, the objectives and/or design of the exchanges, the topics addressed, and the limited access to resources and/or tools for analysis that would provide impetus and knowledge for richer discussions. Lecturers or students may not be willing or prepared to face potentially uncomfortable issues (Glimäng, 2022; Helm, 2015; Ware & Kramsch, 2005) and may intentionally avoid them. In describing her exchange, King de Ramirez, for example, writes that, 'Instructors were careful to not assign discussion topics that may be polemic and polarizing for the student groups involved (e.g. immigration, border security, etc.)' (King De Ramirez, 2021, p. 88). This seems somewhat contradictory since the VE addressed the divisive theme of migration and later she writes that the exchange was in line with critical pedagogies that challenge learners 'to identify, analyze, and relearn their understanding of the world' (King De Ramirez, 2021, p. 88). Other approaches to VE that see conflict and disorienting dilemmas as opportunities for learning and transformation to occur will be discussed in Section 5.

To conclude this section, it is important to consider how we define culture in our VE and the extent to which we equate culture with nation. It is useful to remember that people belong to and identify with diverse groups and communities, not just a nation-state. One way of complexifying the concepts of culture, nation and identity in VE is by making salient the multiple identities that students have and their relevance in different contexts. Historical and political dimensions can be introduced to a VE through the choice of topics and the use of texts and resources that allow students to engage more critically with the concepts of culture and identity. This is important, for identity constructions connect historical memory with contemporary experience, creating narratives that help people navigate the social world (Alcoff, 2011).

4 Challenge-Based Approaches

The last two decades have seen an exponential growth in challenge-based learning (CBL) in higher education at various levels (Gallagher & Savage, 2023; Malmqvist et al., 2015). CBL has been described as:

> a learning experience where the learning takes place through the identification, analysis and design of a solution to a sociotechnical problem. It is typically multidisciplinary, takes place in an international context and aims to find a solution, which is environmentally, socially and economically sustainable. (Malmqvist et al., 2015, p. 1)

In CBL, students are presented with complex and often interdisciplinary challenges that require them to apply their knowledge, critical thinking, creativity, and collaboration skills to develop solutions. The challenges posed to students may span multiple subject areas, requiring the integration of knowledge and skills from various disciplines to develop solutions. Challenges tackled in CBL often have global significance, such as environmental issues, social justice, and public health, which call for an understanding of global interconnectedness and cultural diversity. The term CBL is often used interchangeably with terms such as project-based learning and problem-based learning (PBL), though specific frameworks, definitions, and approaches to CBL have been developed (Gallagher & Savage, 2023). It is beyond the scope of this Element to define these different approaches to learning – within which there are many different schools of thought and practices. What the approaches have in common is that they are forms of active learning and represent a move in higher education to more student-centred, collaborative and inquiry-based approaches to teaching and learning. All three approaches are being applied also in the design of VEs, particularly in the fields of business and management, global citizenship, global health, and STEM.

In CBL students are often placed in what are known as 'global virtual teams' in the field of business and management, which are defined as:

> work arrangements where team members from geographically dispersed places work interdependently to achieve common goals, using electronic media, online collaboration tools, and project management software. (Karabati, 2022, p. 28)

Global virtual teams (GVTs) have become a rich area of research this century, due to their importance and the advantages that effective GVTs bring to multinational businesses and organisations (Cogburn et al., 2010; Cogburn & Levinson, 2008; Tavoletti & Taras, 2023). Businesses have been keen on using virtual teams as they allow them to save money on travel expenses and logistics, they allow for greater flexibility in the face of global competition (working 24 hours), they provide better access to talent and technical experts, and proximity to customers across the globe (Taras, 2022a). Researchers have focused on the specificity and dynamics of GVTs that result from the combination of global/international work, teamwork, and virtual work. It is argued that the intersection of these three dimensions requires them to be explored together, yet much of the existing literature on cross-cultural communication is based on in-person contexts. 'Cross-cultural issues' have been identified as one of the main themes explored in the GVT literature, together with, and often in relation to, communication, technology, performance, and trust (Taras, 2022a). Furthermore, as discussed in Section 2.4 of this Element, the mediating role of technology on communications and 'cultures-of-use' has an impact on intercultural communication, also in GVTs.

Virtual exchange is seen as offering an experiential approach to understanding international collaboration and working in GVTs and has been embraced above all in international business education but also other fields and in interdisciplinary exchanges. Challenge-based VEs have been developed on a large scale, with some projects involving multiple partners located in many different countries. The examples I present in this section are X-Culture and the NICE project. The former is a long-standing, large-scale VE, probably the best known in international business education, and has generated a vast amount of data and research literature. The NICE project also involves multiple partners but is on a smaller, European scale and addresses societal challenges, bringing together students from a range of disciplines. In addition, CBL and PBL have been adopted in projects with only two or three partners. As examples, I introduce two bilateral VEs involving partners in the global north and south in the fields of global health and sustainable development.

4.1 X-Culture

The X-Culture Project is a large-scale VE in the field of international business studies that was established in 2010 by Vas Taras.[25] It started as an educational project with students from different countries working in international online teams to solve a challenge. The aim, as stated on the website is 'preparing students for global careers and effective performance in the multi-culture workplace'.[26] The first iteration of the project involved around 400 students from 7 different countries, since then it has grown exponentially – in 2018 an estimated 5,000 students from over 140 universities in 40 countries on 6 continents participated in X-Culture each semester.[27] The project has expanded and involves corporate partners, with companies now identifying challenges for students to solve in GVTs. The project has also expanded in terms of research, with data generated from the project made available to researchers interested in collaborating in the research (Taras, 2022b).

---

[25] https://x-culture.org/.   [26] https://x-culture.org/for-researchers/.
[27] https://x-culture.org/wp-content/uploads/2018/02/Module-1.-The-X-Culture-Project-Purpose-History-Method-Vision-.pdf.

The types of challenges students are asked to solve often relate to the expansion of the market or increase in revenue of specific businesses, as we see in the examples below:

> Product: Simulations and games for business students
> Challenge: The company designs online games and simulations to aid business education. It already works with dozens of universities in Brazil and neighboring countries, and seeks to expand its market globally. The company asks for your help with identifying new promising markets, and developing a market entry and promotion strategy.

> Product: Airport
> Challenge: The airport asks for help with developing a strategy for increasing its non-aeronautical revenue, increasing the number of passengers, and improving passenger experiences.[28]

Students are provided with detailed information about the companies that present the challenge, the context and goals of the company and the challenge itself. They are required to work for eight weeks in teams of five to eight people, each from a different country, and complete various activities such as industry and competition analysis, new market selection and analysis, identification of promotion channels, messaging, and development of materials. These are then to be presented to the company and academics in the form of a collaboratively written structured report. Before beginning the collaborative teamwork students take part in pre-project training which includes information on the consulting process, and modules about working in GVTs covering issues such as team leadership, coordination, communication, and conflict resolution.

The premise on which the project is based is that:

> Collaboration among people from different countries, cultures, organizations, and institutional environments presents numerous advantages; the diversity of perspectives and knowledge pools greatly enhances the team's creativity and decision-making. However, such workgroups often have to deal with time-zone differences, limited in-person contact substituted by communication online, and the differences stemming from cultural and institutional diversity, which presents challenges not experienced by traditional collocated teams. (Tavoletti & Kochkina, 2022 – back cover of handbook)

Reflecting discourse often found in the field of business, the text above presents the diversity of cultures as adding value to collaboration in virtual teams, bringing greater creativity, a variety of perspectives, and knowledge to the task at hand. Cultural diversity is defined above all in terms of the different nationalities of students taking part in the project (Tavoletti & Kochkina, 2022).

---

[28] https://x-culture.org/2019-2a/.

Participants are positioned as members of a GVT, and their national culture is seen as relevant in so far as it brings diversity and creativity to the group through the different values and cultural knowledge and practices they may have, as can be read in the text below from the X-Culture handbook:

> X-culture teams are relatively diverse. Members usually come from four or five different countries and, although they are likely to have similar educational backgrounds they tend to differ in their values. Always keep in mind that the customs and traditions of different nations and regions may help the team reduce groupthink and improve collective creativity. Try to utilize diversity to the benefit of the team and the project. (Karabati, 2022, p. 31)

Cultural diversity is seen as positive as it can limit 'groupthink', that is, when the tendency of group members to seek concurrence becomes dominant and hinders the possibility to think of alternative solutions or ways forward (Karabati, 2022). This may occur because group members want to avoid conflict, or it may also be due to power dynamics. At the same time, cultural diversity is presented as a challenge to be overcome as cross-cultural issues and misunderstandings together with online communication and limited contact can prevent groups from meeting their objectives. Issues related to cultural diversity are seen to have a negative impact on 'performance', that is, they can hinder successful collaboration and the identification of solutions. X-culture seeks to address this notion of cultural diversity as a challenge through research, which is shared with students and coaches. As reported on the webpage for researchers:

> X-Culture has also emerged as a unique and versatile research platform. We primarily focus on exploring the nature and challenges of cross-cultural collaboration, as well as studying the processes and performance in global virtual teams. What helps and what hurts international workgroup dynamics? Why? What can be done to improve performance in the global workplace?[29]

A bibliometric analysis identified 'cross-cultural issues' as one of the main themes addressed in research studies on GVTs, together with trust – the difficulty in building trust in GVTs, the performance of teams, and issues related to communication, and technology (Tavoletti & Taras, 2023). The main theoretical framework on culture and intercultural communication cited in research publications linked to X-Culture is, unsurprisingly, Hofstede's (2001), which was briefly outlined in Section 2.2. Taras and collaborators specify that 'despite the many concerns, Hofstede's framework has largely defined how we conceptualise and measure culture' (Taras et al., 2023, p. 2). The concerns regard above all the psychometric qualities of Hofstede's work, but researchers have developed

---

[29] https://x-culture.org/for-researchers/.

similar quantitative frameworks that use questionnaires to study and measure cultural/national values and differences for use in international business training programmes.

4.2 The NICE Programme

A similar project to X-Culture but on a much smaller scale is the NICE programme[30] (Network for Intercultural Competence to Facilitate Entrepreneurship) which aims to develop intercultural and entrepreneurial skills among students through VE and collaborative projects. This too embodies a functional, convergent approach to intercultural communication with students working in diverse virtual teams to design a solution to a challenge.[31] As we can read on the project website,[32] the programme is framed in terms of employability and entrepreneurship, 'building skills to enhance employability' and 'encouraging entrepreneurship', one of the objectives of the European Commission. Developing intercultural competence and effective collaboration are seen as key to employability in the global marketplace. Students are thus positioned as future workers or entrepreneurs in a globalised job market for which they need to acquire these necessary competences and skills. In the project they will be team members and problem-solvers, 'creative, innovative risk-takers who have the ability to plan and manage projects to achieve success'.[33]

As in the X-Culture discourse, there is a focus on performance with emphasis on 'working together' and 'working better', and an alignment with a multicultural ideology that values diversity as an asset, but also considers it as a challenge. As we see in the text below, culture is presented as complex, and part of larger structures. Students need to overcome the challenges of diversity, as we infer from the text that students need to learn how to work with people from other cultures in a 'positive and productive manner':

> We aim to help students develop skills to identify how complex culture and communication structures influence their own lives and consequently how to work with people from other cultures in a positive and productive manner.

The discourse on the website also appeals to a sense of global citizenship and social responsibility by stating, for example, that students will 'build a business

---

[30] www.nice-eu.org/.

[31] The programme was developed in 2018 by eight partner universities that collaboratively designed the exchange. Initially funded by the European Commission, the programme has continued with additional partners involved. Each university partner brings several students, who may come from different disciplinary fields. Unlike X-Culture this project is interdisciplinary, which introduces an additional element of 'diversity' in terms of disciplinary knowledge and experience.

[32] www.nice-eu.org/about-the-project.   [33] www.nice-eu.org/about-the-project.

solution to a Global Challenge – to help make the world a better place'. This aligns with contemporary discourse in global citizenship education around sustainability and ethical considerations. The students have to choose from three societal challenges, based on those identified by the European Commission for the Horizon2020 programme and linked to the Sustainable Development Goals. The three broad challenges are:

- Health, wellbeing, and changing societies;
- Climate action, environment, and resources; and
- Inclusive, innovative, and reflective societies.

Students are then presented with ideas, case studies and specific questions to help them think about their group's 'solution' to the challenge. For example, in relation to the climate challenge they are asked:

- What social enterprise would you create to recycle materials/encourage people to recycle?
- How could you reduce food waste in an innovative way?
- How can you make societies more resilient to climate change?

At the same time as they start working in small groups on the global challenge, students follow a series of online modules through which they learn about entrepreneurship and how to manage culture and diversity.[34] The NICE project uses, amongst other resources, Erin Meyer's Culture Map (Meyer, 2014) which was developed in and for the business world. In a similar vein to Hofstede's work, her Culture Map identifies eight key measurable dimensions that capture cultural, aka national variations in terms of values, communication styles, and business practices of individuals and organisations. Through the modules they are encouraged to learn about how miscommunication occurs and how empathy and listening might improve. They are also introduced to the impact of different communication styles on conversation processes and to understand this as a potential source of conflict. They are led to identify their own preferred communication style and adapt this in order to communicate effectively with their team members. Each group has to formulate several possible propositions and select one to develop collaboratively into their solution. At the end of the project, they are asked to reflect on the experiences they had, the intercultural issues encountered when working in a team and to identify possible stumbling blocks in intercultural communication (NICE, 2020).

In the discourses and framing of both the X-Culture and NICE project the aim is for students to converge on a single solution to the challenge proposed and

---

[34] www.nice-eu.org/nice-training-programme.

collaboratively formulate a report where this solution is outlined. Diversity is welcomed as bringing in greater creativity in identifying solutions but it is also seen as a potential obstacle to the 'performance' of the group. Diversity is thus another challenge to be managed or overcome and training modules are used to prepare students for this by raising their awareness of different values or communication styles and providing strategies for working 'better' in GVTs.

4.3 'North-South' Small-Scale Challenge-Based Virtual Exchanges

Both X-Culture and the NICE project are large-scale VEs involving multiple partners and students working in GVTs. In the former, the teams comprise students from possibly all continents, while the NICE project is strictly European in terms of the partnership, though individual students may come from anywhere in the world. In the following section, I outline two smaller-scale bilateral VE projects which partner students at universities in the United States with students at universities in the 'global south' to work collaboratively to address a challenge related to global health and sustainable development. The information about the projects is drawn not from project websites, but published research on the projects.

Challenge-based learning is seen as a powerful approach to learning about interdependence in the field of global health. Bowen et al. (2021) report on a VE in Global Health designed to connect twenty-four students enrolled in a global health course in the United States with twenty-four students of similar age enrolled in a comparable global health course in Lebanon. Students worked in teams of six students, three from each country, and together sought to identify, study, and address problems Syrian refugees were facing at a camp in the Beqaa Valley in Lebanon, where the Lebanese partner university has been providing various forms of humanitarian assistance in partnership with UNHCR, aid agencies, national ministries, and local NGOs. Through Virtual Reality viewers the students at both sites were able to analyse conditions at the camp. Subsequently, the student groups had to choose a challenge from the following areas:

• education;
• mental health;
• reproductive health; and
• geriatric health.

In developing their solutions, the multilateral teams also collaborated with local partner institutions that were embedded in the community and had working ties to national and international organisations. Furthermore, they consulted experts in both countries and together they investigated the problem and worked to develop and propose a solution to the challenge they had chosen. According to the authors, the students appreciated the 'bidirectionality of programming', that is, learning from counterparts and advisors from different backgrounds, which one student expressed as 'mutual gain'. This gain, however, was different for the two groups, as their strengths were seen as distinct but overlapping and complementary, reproducing the dynamics of international humanitarian work where:

> International actors typically bring technical expertise accumulated through repeated humanitarian relief efforts around the world. Local actors bring expertise on specific needs and particular context, which vary widely from place to place and is crucial to understand. (Bowen et al., 2021, p. 8)

STEM is another disciplinary area in which CBL and PBL are used, though still to a limited extent through VE. Abrahamse et al. (2015) report on a VE entitled Rural Sustainability in Latin America (RSLA) involving a United States (Siena University) and a Bolivian university (Universidad Privada Boliviana (UPB)) in Cochabamba, and a third partner, not directly involved in the exchange – a rural Bolivian university (Unidad Academica Campesina (UAC)). The project adopted a problem-based and service-learning approach, whereby the needs of UAC were posed as problems/challenges for the other students to find solutions for. The premise on which it was based is that sustainable development projects that comprise partnerships between 'developed nations' and 'target populations' often face challenges in collaboration that can be supported by intermediate partners 'who can serve as a cultural bridge between the developed nations and the target populations while being empowered to enact positive change in their own country' (Abrahamse et al., 2015, n.p.). In the VE, students at UPB were positioned as intermediate partners for US students engaging in development projects in Bolivia, 'cultural ambassadors', as the authors state. The students were organised into multidisciplinary teams with members from both universities in each team and were assigned a problem in one of four areas relevant to the needs of the UAC:

- waste/trash management at the UAC and in the surrounding community;
- development of ecotourism at the UAC;
- liquid and solid waste treatment from a small pig farm on the UAC premises; and
- evaluation of alternative energy options for the UAC.

As well as attending co-taught lectures and completing assignments related to the course materials, each group was responsible for researching solutions and creating a report proposing one or a combination of recommendations for the UAC.

The global health and sustainability projects are similar in various respects, not least the nature of the partnerships. They both involve a country in the so-called global north and one in the global south, as well as external partners to the exchange, whose problems the students are seeking solutions for. Furthermore, in both exchanges the challenges are located in the global south, and the students there are positioned as cultural informants or intermediaries, though they may not be directly affected by the challenge discussed.

4.4 Opportunities

Challenge-based approaches offer opportunities for the kind of experiential, intercultural learning that is valued in workplaces and by funding institutions such as the European Commission. It is argued that the emphasis on addressing challenges that transcend borders nurtures a sense of global citizenship (UNESCO, 2014). Students become more aware of their role in the world, their responsibility to diverse communities, and the need for collaborative solutions. The iterative process that CBL requires encourages students to incorporate feedback from peers with diverse perspectives, enhancing the quality of their solutions. It should also provide opportunities to reflect on group dynamics, power imbalances, and equity considerations, which can contribute to a deeper understanding of intercultural teamwork.

Many researchers report students' appreciation of learning from working in GVTs with peers of different backgrounds. The fact that students experience first-hand the challenges of intercultural communication has been found to allow them to create more realistic expectations with respect to intercultural and international virtual collaboration (Bowen et al., 2021; Cogburn et al., 2010; Cogburn & Levinson, 2008; Tavoletti & Taras, 2023; Zwerg-Villegas & Martínez-Díaz, 2016). Working on real-world challenges with a GVT and, in some cases with businesses is an important professionalising experience. Participation in challenge-based VEs has been found to reduce perceived differences among cultures due to the focus on a common goal and the development of cultural intelligence. In an experimental study, Zwerg-Villegas and Martínez-Díaz found that their Colombian students were hesitant to participate in the X-Culture project for fear of being judged by their peers due to the negative reputation of Colombia. However, they concluded that by the end of the exchange 'even if their teammates did hold this preconception, it was easily overcome and that the team goal superseded any initial prejudices' (Zwerg-Villegas & Martínez-Díaz, 2016, p. 14). This result is attributed to the impact of working on a common goal with others from distinct nationalities and cultural backgrounds, through which students gained cultural intelligence, thus reducing stereotyping and biases. While participants expect cultural differences to be a challenge before a project starts, at the end of the project many attribute tensions to factors other than cultural issues. In relation to the X-Culture project, for example, Taras (2022a) found that at the end of the project the percentage of participants that indicate cultural differences as having been a big or very big challenge had dropped from 78 per cent at the outset of the project to 12 per cent. The researchers found that rather than cultural differences, tensions arose largely due to issues such as lack of commitment, low technical skills, language skills, or personal circumstances. In short, the effect of cultural differences has been found to be less significant in team dynamics than many people expect (Taras, 2022a).

Challenge-based VEs that address issues such as the environmental crisis, global health issues, and poverty can be opportunities for increasing knowledge about these themes and understanding the impact on people in different regions through direct engagement. Furthermore, critically framed VEs could be a valuable tool to raise awareness of the responsibilities and complicities of individuals, businesses, and governments in contributing to such challenges. At the same time, there are several potential risks, as will be discussed further.

4.5 Limitations and Risks

There is a tension in the literature on cultural diversity in CBL between the celebration of diversity and the challenges of diversity in teams. The 'bright side' of heightened creativity, is often overshadowed by what is seen as the 'dark side' of cultural differences, that is, the costs and risks produced by cultural barriers (Tavoletti & Taras, 2023, p. 27). There is also a tension between foregrounding cultural differences on the one hand and minimising differences on the other. Focusing on diversity can lead to the reification, pathologisation, and/or romaniticization of difference. On the other hand, minimising difference and supporting the belief that *we are all the same after all* does little to support understanding of historical contexts, structural inequities, and reinforces the 'hegemonic desire of the North for unity and homogeneity' (Souza, 2019). In diverse groups, the differences that are suppressed are usually those of less represented or historically marginalised groups (Ely & Thomas, 2020).

A commonly reported issue in the VE literature in relation to project-based and challenge-based VEs is the focus on the solution/task/product with little time dedicated for interpersonal exchanges or 'social integration', which comprises cohesiveness, trust, and morale (Richter et al., 2021). Research on the X-Culture project, in fact, has found that many of the GVTs do not 'harness the power' in the diversity of the team. Taras (2022a) reports that researchers observed that 74 per cent of teams wasted the opportunity they had to interact and put diverse minds together in brainstorming questions and developing ideas, which is believed to fuel 'collective wisdom'. Rather they tend to divide the workload by sharing out questions among individuals and then combining individual answers or report sections. This approach was identified as a problem by a small percentage of the teams, and though teachers and coaches point out that they are missing out on collective wisdom and not using the best strategy, the teams still fail to adopt this approach. This is perhaps linked to the focus on finding solutions – or in the case of PBL in the creation of a final product. The emphasis is on the development of solutions or strategies that will address a challenge effectively and socialisation or exploring cultural diversity can be perceived as a distraction or waste of time. Functional, skills-focused and solution-oriented approaches to interculturality are seen to reflect the neoliberal paradigm characterising higher education (Marginson, 2022) due to the focus on developing the employability of individual students.

The belief that diversity is a challenge and can be overcome with training about national cultures or communication styles is the premise on which much of the intercultural training industry for businesses is based (Piller, 2017) and is also found in VEs in this field. Many of the resources used for intercultural training in X-Culture are based on the work of Hofstede and others, whose quantitative approaches to the measurement of value orientations often equate culture with national identity. Thus, whilst the exchange itself may bring a diversity of perspectives to address a challenge, the training materials used may reinforce dominant Eurocentric views of the world. This will be the case if the materials are based on oversimplified dichotomous dimensions which do not address the complexity and multifaceted nature of identities in intercultural communication, as already discussed in Section 2.2. There is also the risk of attributing to culture, challenges that are not related to cultural factors, but rather related to language, technology, institutional contexts, and recognition of the work done. All of these dimensions can contribute to imbalances in power, which may stem from multiple causes, and can lead to negative 'performance' in relation to finding solutions to tasks, the key concern of businesses. Furthermore, they can also reproduce coloniality and reinforce bias by ignoring issues of representation and privilege, racism, and classism (Ferri, 2022; Imperiale et al., 2021).

Language has been identified as a source of tension and unequal power dynamics in VE (Deardorff, 2022; O'Dowd, 2023). Research on X-Culture has found that differences in language proficiency can lead to tensions, particularly in groups where there are very different levels of proficiency (Panina, 2022). Where levels are more similar, even if they are all 'low proficiency' this does not tend to be a problem, according to Taras (2022a). Recommendations have been made to rely more on written communication than synchronous video, which is less challenging for less proficient users of English and can 'level the playing field' in X-Culture (Panina, 2022). The language of the exchange is not explicitly mentioned in either of the smaller-scale studies presented above on global health and sustainability, thus we can assume that it is English. Indeed the use of English for VE is often so taken for granted that it is not even mentioned. Yet in an exchange where one of the partners or team members is in the United States or another anglophone country, this can lead to a power imbalance and insecurity on the part of some participants (Guth & Helm, 2017). In the project described earlier on sustainability, Abrahamse et al. (2015) report that Bolivian students were seen as being shyer about speaking and attributed this to cultural differences, without making any reference to the language of the exchange. Yet this shyness is quite likely to have been related to language as they were speaking in what is for them a foreign language to 'native speakers' of that language. Furthermore, as mentioned in Section 2.5, linguistic proficiency constrains the way identity is performed and language choice is a key dimension of power in intercultural communication (Piller, 2017).

Stereotypes and prejudice are key issues in GVTs and relate to power dynamics. In research on the X-Culture project, this has been explored by looking at the country-of-origin (COO) effect in peer evaluations – which are a key component of their project. In a quantitative study based on a sample of 6634 GVTs, which comprised 33,271 people in seventy-nine countries, Tavoletti et al. (2022) found that the prestige and the level of economic development of a team member's COO is a better predictor of peer evaluations than objective measures of individual skills and competencies, including English proficiency, technical ability, and cultural intelligence. This suggests that a COO effect based on personal bias may affect performance ratings more than team members' actual contributions. Furthermore, they found that these effects are present not just at the outset of the project but continue over time as team members continue to collaborate. The authors of the study assert that, 'Indeed, it is not what you know or can do, but where you are from that matters most in peer evaluations in GVTs' (Tavoletti et al., 2022, p. 11) and conclude that this should be taken into account when designing evaluation systems and discussing implications for research and practice. Whilst acknowledging the problem, there appears to be little reflection on the origins and impact of what is essentially a colonial bias and racism, though it is not named as such, and there seems to be no consideration of how this should be addressed in the VE itself. Decolonial scholars point out that Eurocentric worldviews and canons of knowledge have for centuries been regarded by many as the only legitimate way of thinking about the world (Heleta & Chasi, 2022, 2024; Souza, 2022; Souza & Duboc, 2021). It is thus perhaps not surprising that those who come from these bastions of knowledge and power are evaluated more highly regardless of their contribution. However, there are growing movements to counter this 'geopolitics of knowledge' (Mignolo, 2002) and 'epistemic racism' (Grosfoguel, 2015), both within and outside of universities in the global south and the north (Bhambra et al., 2018).

The risk of reproducing colonial dynamics is particularly high in CBL where students in the western world/global north are tasked with finding solutions to problems in the global south. Development work is rife with the 'white saviour complex' (Cole, 2012), which can be easily reproduced in VE. It can occur, for example, in projects where the partners from the global north are positioned as experts tasked with identifying, analysing, and finding solutions to challenges in the global south. The partners in the global south are positioned as key informants and asked to provide information and/or data on the context but are not involved in identifying and analysing the challenges or in identifying possible solutions. In research collaborations this leads to what is defined as an 'extractivist' or 'parasitic' research approach, which has characterised many research partnerships between the global north and south. Researchers from highly resourced countries do research and extract data from typically low-resource settings without establishing equitable collaborations with their partners (Odeny & Bosurgi, 2022). Important considerations thus regard the identification and framing of challenges or problems to be addressed in a VE, the nature of the partnership and the respective roles of participants. Questions need to be raised such as who identified the challenge and who is finding solutions for whom, as well as the broader question of who and whose knowledges are being excluded from the challenge/solution.

5 Dialogue-Based Approaches

The last model of VE that I explore in this Element is dialogue-based VE, which has origins in the fields of conflict resolution and international education. The word 'dialogue' has multiple meanings, and the phrase 'intercultural dialogue' is frequently used as a synonym of intercultural communication. However, here dialogue is used to refer to a specific form of interaction. Dialogic approaches to intercultural learning have been developed and implemented in a range of educational settings in order to further understanding between diverse groups, or groups in conflict with one another. These approaches draw on theory from areas such as post-critical theory and critical pedagogy (Freire, 1970), postcolonial (Spivak, 1999) and postmodern studies (Burbules, 2006), cultural studies (Bhabha, 1994), and peace studies (Lederach, 1995). According to Freire (1970):

> dialogue cannot be reduced to the act of one person's 'depositing' ideas in another, nor can it become a simple exchange of ideas to be 'consumed' by the discussants. Nor yet is it a hostile, polemical argument between those who are committed neither to the naming of the world, not to the search for truth, but rather to the imposition of their own truth. (p. 70)

In practices such as Intergroup Dialogue (Nagda & Gurin, 2007) and Sustained Dialogue (Saunders, 2001), dialogue is seen as interaction that is not coercive or confrontational, but which is instead collaborative and leads to a mutual learning process with participants working together in order to seek understanding of one another. Saunders (1999) developed a practice of 'sustained dialogue', in which through engaging in multiple interactions participants develop relationships and deepen their understanding of each other. This process occurs in several stages, starting with the creation of a safe space where participants can feel secure enough to fully engage in dialogue to better understand previously unfamiliar cultures. The aim is for participants to undergo a transformation and in the final stages they are led to identify ways they can act together to reshape the larger community (Saunders, 1999).

Many dialogue-based education programmes are based on Allport's (1954) contact hypothesis which suggests that interactions between members of 'opposing' groups should be promoted to reduce prejudice and improve intergroup relations (Paolini et al., 2018). According to Allport's (1954) original theory, certain conditions should be met for optimal contact, that is, equal status, common goals, no intergroup competition, and sanction from authorities. Key to the dialogue process is the role of a multipartial facilitator, whose role is to support a constructive exchange by building trust in the group, facilitate mutual learning and participation of all participants, prevent disrespect and confrontation but also conflict avoidance and political correctness which are also barriers to the dialogue process (Tyszblat, 2019). The notion of 'conflict transformation' contrasts with conflict resolution and conflict management. Resolution implies that conflict is negative and should be ended, while management suggests that conflict situations need to be kept under control. Conflict transformation, as defined by Lederach (1995, 2003), recognises conflict as a natural part of social life and human relations and sees it as a way of changing relations and images of the self and others. Paulo Freire, also saw conflict as an agent of change. Transformation thus suggests a dynamic understanding that conflict can move in destructive or constructive directions but proposes an effort to maximise the achievement of constructive, mutually beneficial processes and outcomes.

Dialogue-based VE is not widespread in higher education. The two cases I report on are well-established models of dialogue-based VE that have been developed and are implemented by the NGOs Soliya[35] and Sharing Perspectives Foundation,[36] which partner with higher education institutions to offer students the opportunity to participate. I have selected them because they are large-scale VEs with partners in a wide range of contexts, and a fairly substantial body of research has been carried out on these, in particular the Soliya Connect Program (Bruneau et al., 2020; Helm et al., 2012; Helm, 2013, 2016, 2018a; Nolte-Laird, 2022). Furthermore, I am familiar with both cases, having been involved with them in multiple guises: as an educator with students participating in the exchanges since 2009, as a dialogue facilitator as well as a researcher.

5.1 The Soliya Connect Program

Just two years after 9/11 and the beginning of George Bush's War on Terror, Soliya's Connect Program (SCP) was designed in 2003 to address the tensions between 'Western' and 'predominantly Arab and Muslim' societies, and to provide 'a deeper understanding of the perspectives of others on important socio-political issues and crucial 21st Century skills, including critical thinking, communication, and digital media literacy'.[37] The historical and socio-political context in which the project was developed is important as it defined the dividing line on which the programme was originally developed and the target groups, who were students in the United States and Middle East and North African countries. Since then, the target audience and the programming have expanded to include European countries and also other parts of the world.[38] Significantly the SCP has also been taken up on a local level to address internal socio-political divisions within the United States, in particular on university campuses with the programme being adopted as part of orientation activities and professional development for students and university leaders.[39]

SCP is based on principles of intergroup contact and sustained dialogue between members of 'opposing groups'. It is also informed by research on the impact of media on intergroup relations (Argo et al., 2009), their polarising influence on relations across cultures, but at the same time a belief that media

---

[35] www.soliya.net.   [36] https://sharingperspectivesfoundation.com/.
[37] https://soliya.net/connect-program.   [38] https://soliya.net/connect-program-partners.
[39] https://soliya.net/first-year-connect.

can have a constructive impact on how people perceive and address global issues. On the homepage of Soliya's website we read:

> We envision a pluralistic world where diversity is embraced and conflicts are transformed into opportunities for collaboration and collective learning. For 20 years, we have taught young adults to approach differences constructively and lead with empathy, so that we all may thrive in an interconnected, pluralistic world.[40]

Though the word 'culture' does not appear in this text, diversity is the focus of the project and there is an explicit recognition of conflict. However, unlike the VEs explored in the previous sections, neither conflict nor diversity are presented as challenges to be overcome, but rather as potential for transformation and learning. Furthermore, the programme does not shy away from potentially divisive issues, but rather makes them the core of the exchange and the dialogue process. The original framing of the Connect Programme around 'Western societies' and 'predominantly Muslim societies' presents a possible tension since the use of broad social group label indexes homogeneity and ignores the political, religious, economic, social, and demographic heterogeneity within these groups. Yet it is used in a strategic way, as defining groups is necessary in order to address intergroup relations, and problematising the labels and the language used to talk about the 'other' is included in the programme activities.

Through the Connect Program, students from a wide range of partner universities in the United States, European countries, southern Mediterranean countries and beyond[41] are placed in small, diverse dialogue groups that meet over a period of eight weeks for two-hour sessions of online facilitated dialogue. The sessions are led by facilitators, often volunteer alumni of the Soliya's Connect Program who have been trained in the implementation of this form of online dialogue. They have gone through two training programmes to equip them to facilitate groups and support them in openly engaging with topics that may be sensitive or even taboo in some contexts. Their role is to create a 'safe space' and to be 'multipartial' as they guide the dialogue process.[42] Facilitation tools include awareness-raising and addressing group dynamics, as well as using active listening skills such as summarising, mirroring, and reframing. Facilitators bring critical thinking to a conversation by asking questions, exploring terminology used, and addressing not only opinions but also actions and feelings (Helm, 2021). Facilitators also have a coach whose role is to provide advice and support and observe sessions, providing feedback and opportunities for developing and improving their skills. Most facilitate on

---

[40] https://soliya.net/.   [41] see partnerships here https://soliya.net/connect-program-partners.
[42] See video on facilitating dialogue www.youtube.com/watch?v=2e01oqLULXo.

a volunteer basis, reflecting their intercultural curiosity and a commitment to promoting constructive dialogue (Helm, 2016; Nolte-Laird, 2022). Ideally, the facilitators in each dialogue group are paired, and where possible there is one from the so-called Western world and another from the predominantly Muslim world, preferably an Arabic speaker, thus able to address power dynamics and language inequalities.

All dialogue groups follow a shared calendar and an online curriculum that has a clear structure and progression. The facilitators plan and lead the sessions, choosing activities from the Soliya curriculum for each week in order to achieve the objectives that the project sets out. The sequence of activities and discussion topics in the curriculum has been intentionally designed to allow participants to get to know one another and feel safe before addressing the more personal and sensitive issues. In the first session, the themes addressed are: the nature of dialogue and how it differs from debate and discussion, identifying global and social challenges and issues in their communities:

- What do you think are the most pressing global and social challenges in the world today? What are the most pressing issues in your country /community? How do those two sets of challenges compare?
- How and why do different countries and regions perceive global and social challenges differently? What do you think of the issues your peers raised that were different from your own?[43]

In the second week, they take part in activities that allow them to explore issues related to identity and are encouraged to think about how their identity and experiences affected their understanding of and perspective on these issues and on global challenges. Culture is thus linked to participants' identities and their experiences. The activities facilitators set up for them are designed to make multiple dimensions of participants' identities emerge (Helm, 2018a). The curriculum also includes materials and a dialogue session on the topic of intercultural communication, which is explored by participants being asked to define culture, engage with concepts such as ethnocentrism and cultural relativism, talking about what they see as challenges to communication across cultures, their impact, and how they can address such challenges.

The dialogue group, which normally comprises eight to twelve participants from different contexts, is a key component of the programme, and over the weeks of the exchange participants get to know one another better and a group identity develops, and the groups themselves begin to choose what issues they

---

[43] Soliya Virtual Exchange Implementation Manual for Connect Global, Spring 2024 – a document shared with educators implementing the SCP with their students.

want to engage with in certain weeks of the programme. These include emerging and new technologies, immigration/integration, culture, and stereotypes, the role of religion in society and personal lives, media (traditional, online, social, etc.), environment and natural resources, current events, social movements, inequality, health, and gender issues. Participants are encouraged to engage with these topics on a deep level with the support of the facilitators and to go beyond transactional exchanges. Over the weeks, activities are included to allow members to get to know each other on a deeper, more personal level. A key session is one in which participants share 'Life Stories' and are asked questions such as:

- What experiences in your life have been most important in terms of making you the person that you are today?
- How have your life experiences affected your worldview and your political perspective?

This particular session is key to supporting group members to recognise how different personal experiences can lead to different worldviews and can encourage them to hear the perspective of 'the other side' by re-thinking their experience and frames of reference. However, this session cannot take place until group members have developed a level of trust within the group. In the final session, participants take part in activities in which they collectively reflect on their group's experience and acknowledge what they have learnt from their peers during the exchange. Whilst students are encouraged to reflect individually in weekly journals the group reflection, which is led by the facilitator, is key to validating one another and the collective learning process. In this session, they also formulate ideas as to how they (both as individuals and as a group) can address the challenges they have been exploring at multiple levels, from the local to the global. This final step moves them towards a future orientation, and to use Byram's (2008) terms, from the pre-political (i.e. engaging with others and reflecting critically on their own and others' assumptions and imagining possible alternatives) to the political (taking action to foster change).

5.2 Sharing Perspectives: Cultural Encounters

The Sharing Perspectives Foundation (SPF) has developed VEs that combine this type of sustained, facilitated dialogue with rich video and text-based content on issues that are often seen as divisive or controversial, such as migration, politics, gender and media, and climate justice. The SPF define themselves as 'a not-for-profit offering contemporary online learning experiences for people to interact across divides, whether national, cultural, social, or political'.[44] Culture is

---

[44] https://sharingperspectivesfoundation.com/we-stand-for/.

mentioned as one of several dividing lines, together with the national, social, and political. Again, the attitude to difference is to recognise it as a dividing line, however not one to be overcome but rather to embrace. As we read on their website, VE is framed as an 'inclusive pedagogical approach' used to offer people a 'meaningful international and cross-cultural experience'. Based in Europe, SPF has worked mainly on EC-funded projects involving students from European and South Mediterranean countries. They specify that they see conflict and divergence in opinions as potential opportunities for learning. The emphasis is thus not on convergence or on specific outcomes, but rather the process of dialogue:

> We value diversity as a strength and appreciate difference. We do not believe that reaching consensus is an objective of learning or exchange. We are curious while being critical. We see conflict and difference of opinion as an opportunity for learning when addressed constructively. Process is key to that achievement.[45]

Cultural Encounters has been one of SPF's flagship programmes, and has addressed several themes over the years, for example, 'Cultural Encounters: Perspectives on Populism', which was about the rise of populist voices and their often nationalist agendas. The exchange called on students to look at the impact of this on migration policies and migrant rights, people's sense of belonging and processes of exclusion. It thus addressed the controversial themes critical intercultural communication scholars call for, with groups of students located in European and South Mediterranean countries.

Like the SCP, this VE starts with explorations of identities, asking how identities are shaped in pluralised societies and how movements across borders affect understandings of belonging. Over the weeks of exchange, concepts related to populism, democracy, migration, belonging, nationalism, and national identity are explored, first of all through content and individual reflections and then through the weekly dialogue sessions. As in the SCP, the group process is key to the dialogue and participants gradually explore their own and each other's identities, as this reflection from a student journal[46] shows:

> This week the discussion was much more dynamic since the members of the group are starting to know each other, and it was very pleasant. I expect our further discussions to get more and more complex as the topics we talk about also complexify. Last week, I knew we all came from different countries and cultures, but I have learned even more about my classmates: a few of us come from several nationalities at the same time, some of them unexpected and uncommon, and we were able to discuss about that « hybridization », how

---

[45] https://sharingperspectivesfoundation.com/we-stand-for/.
[46] Permission was obtained from participants to use anonymised journal data.

people see us, and how we live with it. Since some of the members actually had trouble with this, especially during their childhood, our meeting room became a sort of support group. I believe this multiculturality makes our group more open-minded and enlarges our perspectives and points of views: to me, this is a clue to richer debates during the next sessions. (cited in Baroni & Helm, forthcoming)

The facilitators are expected to guide students through the phases of dialogue, assessing, and responding to the needs and progression of the group through the process. A framework outlining different phases has been defined to support facilitators, however it is made clear that this is not 'a blueprint' and the process is not linear, groups will vary in the process. Groups generally begin with low levels of trust as they enter a new unknown space, and gradually develop bonds as they identify and explore similarities and common interests and goals. Only as trust builds can the group begin to name and acknowledge differences between them and start to address divisive issues. Once trust is high, the group members should be able to express themselves openly and critically examine their own beliefs and thinking process as well as those of others through attentive and open listening. Toward the end of the exchange the group can move to future-oriented discussions and as they wind down, reflect on the process and the learning they have gone through and decide how to keep in touch.

In both SCP and the Cultural Encounters VEs, culture is linked to participants' identities and experiences, which the dialogue process makes central. These identities are fluid and constantly negotiated as through their interactions the participants position themselves and one another, using categories that they may or may not align to (Helm, 2018a). As well as individual identities, what emerges, or should emerge through the dialogue process is also the small culture of the groups as they establish routines, ways of interacting with one another, and develop a shared history and experience. These small cultures that emerge in each of the groups are unique, but they do share some of the discourses of the broader VE project, a way of engaging with difference, of asking questions, of interacting which is acquired through the activities they have engaged in, the modelling of the facilitators and materials they have shared.

5.3 Opportunities

Scholars have recognised that sensitive and potentially divisive issues should be addressed for meaningful intercultural learning and that tensions ought to be recognised as an inevitable and transformative part of intercultural dialogue rather than as something to be avoided (Helm, 2016; Levine & Phipps, 2012; Schneider & Emde, 2006; Ware & Kramsch, 2005). Yet both students and educators are often reluctant to face such themes, as research has shown (Glimäng, 2022; Helm, 2015, 2016) since they feel it is not their role to engage students in discussion of 'political' issues or they feel they are not equipped to do so. Furthermore, educators have tended to engage with partner classes that are more culturally similar. Educators in the global north tend to partner with classes in the global north, at least in foreign language education (Çiftçi & Savas, 2018; Helm, 2015). Dialogue-based programmes such as SCP and Cultural Encounters directly address these key challenges that have been identified in relation to interculturality, that is, how to get students to engage in deeper levels of interaction (Kramsch & Thorne, 2002; Ware & Kramsch, 2005) and engage in meaningful exchanges where they move beyond the 'assumption of similarity' to an intercultural stance (Ware, 2005).

Both dialogue-based exchanges described earlier entailed north-south partnerships, though the lead organisations in both cases are in the global north. The great diversity of the participants in terms of geopolitical, socio-economic, and cultural backgrounds, has been identified as one of the components of the model which contributes to the deeper levels of engagement and learning on the part of students (Bruneau et al., 2020; Helm & Velden, 2021; Nolte-Laird, 2022). For students in contexts such as Palestine and Syria, places of 'restricted travel' (Imperiale, 2021) it provides an opportunity to break their isolation and have at least 'virtual exposure' to international and intercultural experiences (Al Mqadma & Al Karriri, 2020). As a student participant in SCP commented:

> Living in Gaza under the siege makes it unrealistically hard for me to leave the Gaza strip, which in turn reduces my chance of interacting with students from all over the world. [. . .]I was so excited and keen to join this programme. Since it has always been my dream to leave Gaza Strip and travel around the world to discover more about other cultures and work on my language skills . . . In my sessions, I had six friends from different countries so for me it was a journey to six countries. (cited in Al Mqadma & Al Karriri, 2020)

Both programmes provide students in many regions with direct access to individuals in places they are likely to only have read about in the media since mobility is limited due to geopolitical conflicts, visa regimes, socio-economic status, about which many are likely to have negative stereotypes. Participants are able to 'put a face' to the news they hear about different regions, which often raises interest in knowing more about the context and issues they are facing both through the media and the contacts they have acquired. As a student from the Cultural Encounters project reported, 'although you hear of this [traumatic news]in the newspapers or online, it doesn't become real until you have seen and spoken to someone going through it' (cited in Giralt, 2020).

The SCP and Cultural Encounters programmes have been found valuable for supporting students in understanding their situatedness and how it can influence their positionality, perspectives, and also knowledge about certain issues. A student in a Cultural Encounters exchange highlights this:

> I think the online classroom is a very interesting concept, as it is a way to get connected and learn with people around the world. And specially in studies like migration study or development cooperation I think it is the only way to successfully learn about the topic and to avoid the mistake of having a national centered view on the topics. Of course I needed to get used to the online classroom, as it is my first online course. But with the time it was easier to discuss online. (cited in Baroni & Helm, forthcoming)

Dialogue-based exchanges provide valuable opportunities for multiple identity positionings of participants, which will change even within a single session through the topics addressed, the questions asked, and the process of dialogue. Participants changed their positioning from, for example, language learners insecure of their ability to express themselves to 'experts of their own experiences' (Helm, 2018a). In sharing their knowledge with peers who were interested in acquiring greater understanding of the themes addressed, they claimed voice and power dynamics changed.

Research carried out in the field of social psychology has found that participation in SCP, which is framed as an 'online intergroup contact intervention', is associated with 'a reduction in prejudice, an increase in confidence in communicating in intercultural settings, enhanced self-reported knowledge about Western-Muslim relationships, and a higher likelihood to take collective action on behalf of outgroup members'. (Schumann & Moore, 2022, p. 1083). Furthermore, this longitudinal study found that many of these changes lasted eighteen months after the end of the exchange. Another study in the same field looked at whether intergroup contact through the SCP VE could lead to dehumanisation, a process which is seen as distinct from, but complementary to prejudice, and highly consequential for intergroup conflict (Bruneau et al., 2020). The researchers, who as in the previously cited study used pre- and post-exchange surveys, found that quality of contact was strongly associated with reduction in dehumanisation and meta-dehumanisation, that is, the perception that others dehumanise you (Bruneau et al., 2020). Humanisation of the 'other' was also a finding from an ethnographic study that used both participant observation and interviews, carried out within a peacebuilding framework (Nolte-Laird, 2022). Humanisation here was defined as shifts in perceptions of the 'other' and reduction in stereotypes. This humanisation was seen to be a result of building meaningful relationships with peers through the exchange. Yet she argues that if positive peace is to be an outcome of dialogue programmes, it is important that increased critical consciousness or intentional action accompanies the creation of friendship or positive relations with others. In her research this was the case for most participants, but not all as some participants felt that having participated in the encounter alone is something positive. Nolte-Laird's (2022) research confirms findings from several earlier mixed methods studies which found that engaging in dialogue with people from parts of the world they had previously known mainly or exclusively through the media had an important impact on participants and led them to re-evaluate some of the biases they may have had (Helm, 2013). A recent large-scale study which involved over 5,000 participants compared different models of VE and found that participants' feelings towards people with different ethnic and religious backgrounds improved significantly for students taking part in these dialogue-based exchanges, while there was no significant change for students taking part in other models of VE (Helm & Velden, 2021).

A defining feature of the intercultural learning that takes place through dialogue-based approaches to VE is learning to listen, in particular active listening. This kind of listening is key to relationality, learning from and with others. It requires attentiveness and responsiveness and has been recognised as key to bridging gaps between people (Schultz, 2003), also because *being heard* is critical for groups in conflict. Researchers in conflict resolution have found that different groups have distinct psychological needs. While perspective-taking can improve attitudes towards an out-group for members of dominant groups, it does not have an impact, or can even produce a negative effect on members of non-dominant or disempowered groups. For the latter, perspective-giving is more effective, particularly feeling heard by outgroup members is important for them (Bruneau & Saxe, 2012). Evidence of this has been found in research on the SCP in quantitative studies (Bruneau et al., 2020), but also in qualitative as we see how this participant describes perspective giving:

> During the program time I felt like I was the ambassador for my country, my culture and my people. I had to clarify the real situation in Palestine, Gaza and West Bank. I had to express myself, my feelings during the Intifada. I wasn't surprise[d] by the fact that not all of my friends are familiar with the real situation. Unfortunately, because media is dominated by the major forces in the world, people outside don't know the real situations. (cited in Helm et al., 2012, p. 113)

Through active listening and opening themselves to change participants began to recognise their situatedness and how their education, socio-cultural context, and historical experiences impact their world view. The conversations allowed them to realise their own position of thinking and seeing the world. That is, through their interactions with the other, their locus of enunciation and positionality became visible to them, as seen in the quote below.

> It is amazing that we all can share our opinions at the same time about the same topic. It really opened my eyes because there are people from a lot of countries who made me realise that my point of view is not the only one. I see the world from a Western Europe person point of view, and that is definitely not the only perspective. I could see that each country has a very different way of thinking than me. (cited in Baroni & Helm, forthcoming)

A further intercultural learning outcome that has been found from these dialogue-based programmes is what has been called 'intervention' (Nolte-Laird, 2022) and 'activation' (Helm & Velden, 2021). Intervention is recognised as deliberate and intentional shifts in behaviour and actions, which can be seen as a form of social activism, as defined by Ladegaard and Phipps (2020). In the context of the Erasmus+ Virtual Exchange programme, activation was conceptualised as sharing information about what they were learning with other people, challenging media misrepresentations and seeking further opportunities for intercultural exchange – both online and in-person, and well over two-thirds of research participants were activated in some way. The citation below comes from a participant in a dialogue-based VE:

> I am even more so interested in following through with creating more connections with youths across the globe to build a solidarity platform on how to better address the conflict situations in our different countries. Indeed I have found the courage to connect, to question our failing system and motivation to keep speaking and doing my own bit to transform my society. Peace is possible. (Helm & Velden, 2021, p. 69)

5.4 Limitations and Risks

One of the key limitations of these large-scale VEs is the issue of language and its implications in terms of access, power dynamics and hegemonies. Most dialogue-based exchanges that involve participants from a wide range of contexts employ English as the language for the exchange (Helm, 2015; Helm & Acconcia, 2019; Nolte-Laird, 2022). This certainly prevents many people from accessing such VEs, as though English is often cited as a 'global' language, its reach is limited to a social elite who have access to the language (Pennycook, 2007; Piller, 2016). Even amongst those who have sufficient proficiency and access the exchanges, some may feel an asymmetric power dynamic and may be initially inhibited from speaking, particularly when there are highly proficient speakers in the group and when addressing particularly complex and/or emotional issues (Helm, 2013, 2016; Nolte-Laird, 2022). A further issue is the disengagement of expert speakers who may not have the patience or the experience of interacting with international groups (Bruni, 2020) and thus do not listen actively (Nolte-Laird, 2022). This can result in tensions participants not feeling heard. In the SCP and Cultural Encounters programmes one of the responsibilities of the facilitators is to acknowledge this language imbalance and take steps to support participants by, for example, engaging them in activities that raise awareness of the rich multilingual repertoires of participants, for instance through ice-breaking activities that call different languages into play. Furthermore, checking understanding, paraphrasing and rephrasing are ways of supporting understanding, as is the transcription of what is being said in the text chat. Research findings (Helm, 2013; Helm, 2018a; Helm & Velden, 2021) suggest that this is particularly important in encouraging participants from the Southern Mediterranean countries to speak more, and do so openly, as we see in the citation below in response to an open question:

> in many times students were not able to express there ideas in English and sometimes differences in our accent would not let us understand will but we easily overcame that because of the amazing facilitators we had such as Emma 'the English version of my mind' and Fatima 'she types just what we wonna say': P (cited in Helm, 2013)

However, very much also depends on the quality and professionality of the facilitators and the dynamics of the group. Group dynamics are key to the success of the programme and to individuals' learning yet these are also variable and not completely controllable (Helm & Velden, 2021). There are always risks that not all group members attend the sessions regularly or punctually, or that they are engaged in the sessions. There are multiple possible reasons for this (lack of academic recognition for participation, mandatory participation, temporary lack of connectivity . . .) not all of which can be addressed (Alami et al., 2022). Nonetheless, the impact extends to all members of the dialogue group. Access to technology and bandwidth for video-conferencing is a limitation for many participants, as well as having a quiet and safe space in which they can connect and speak freely. It has been argued by scholars engaging with critical VE (Hauck, 2023) that to be more accessible to a broader group, VEs should use low bandwidth technologies. However, in the case of facilitated dialogue on sensitive and conflictual issues it is argued that seeing one another and engaging in synchronous spoken communication is fundamental (Helm, 2018a; Nolte-Laird, 2022).

Finally, what might be seen as a limitation which is not linked to the learning outcomes, but rather to the implementation of VE at institutions, is the fact that these exchanges are not run by educators themselves, but by external NGOs. It is worth noting that it would be very challenging for academics or single institutions to set up, implement, and monitor exchanges with such a multiplicity of partners, facilitators, and with support and control mechanisms in place to ensure the quality and ethics of the facilitated dialogue. Hence the rationale for external organisations taking on this role, and it is important to point out that these are not-for-profit organisations. For many institutions finding funds to invest in such programmes is a challenge, hence they rely on funding programmes that support their implementation, yet these are not always sustainable over time. Also challenging is finding ways to integrate and provide recognition for these activities in academic curricula (Giralt et al., 2022).

6 Final Remarks

As I have sought to show in this Element, intercultural communication comes in many shapes and forms in VE, with different objectives and learning outcomes for those involved. This has always been the case for intercultural communication and reflects, in part, the interests and concerns of the fields in which intercultural communication has developed: foreign language education, business, health sciences, global citizenship education, and peacebuilding. In all of these areas, VE has been adopted as an experiential approach to intercultural learning. Table 1 summarises the three 'models' to VE as presented and discussed in this Element, highlighting the main activities involved, representations of culture and intercultural communication, opportunities and risks/limitations they may present for intercultural learning.

The three approaches were presented here as distinct, though most VEs comprise elements of more than one. For example, O'Dowd and Ware's (2009) widely adopted Progressive Exchange model of VE entails students' making cultural comparisons and subsequently collaborating on some kind of project or product. Many small-scale COIL VEs are largely project-based with students collaborating in small teams on a project (Rubin & Guth, 2022), but they often also comprise activities which involve making cultural comparisons. Regarding dialogue-based VE, both Soliya and SPF have recently developed programmes which have added a collaborative component. Soliya's Connect Collaborate integrates dialogue with a group project that entails developing an online awareness campaign to address a topic of current relevance and interest.[47] The SPF also have participants collaborate in developing actions or awareness-raising campaigns on issues they address in their VE, such as the recent CliVEx[48] (Climate Virtual Exchange: Enhancing Climate Awareness in

---

[47] https://soliya.net/connect-program.   [48] https://clivex.eu/.

Table 1 Defining features of three models of virtual exchange

	Comparative	Challenge-based	Dialogue-based
Main activity	Engage in cultural comparisons	Work in teams to find solutions to global or business challenges or problems	Engage in weekly, synchronous dialogue sessions
Sample projects	*Cultura*	X-Culture NICE programme	Soliya Connect Program Cultural Encounters
Representation of culture	National cultures and products (statistics, historical documents, media, films. . .) Hidden culture (values, beliefs, and meanings) Culture as related to language Culture as national institutions, education systems	Culture as asset bringing creativity Culture as challenge affecting group performance National culture Small culture of the global virtual team	Broad regional cultures: Western cultures predominantly Arab/ Muslim cultures Cultural diversity as value and enrichment Culture as multiple identities and experiences Small culture of dialogue group
Approach to intercultural communication	Information exchange Hypothesis making Cultural exploration Discussion	Discussion and collaboration Solution or result-oriented Functional, convergent	Dialogue Process-oriented Divergent Active listening and being heard
Opportunities	In-depth explorations of cultural 'rich points'	First-hand experience of challenges of intercultural communication and team work	Engagement with broad diversity of participants and life experiences

	Understand cultural embeddedness of own beliefs and positionality Complexity culture Improved intercultural understanding and communicative competence Exposure to broader set of perspectives Understand how discourses are shaped by historical factors	Realistic expectations of work culture Professionalising experience Reduce perceived differences among cultures Understanding that not only cultural difference lead to challenges in GVT Increased knowledge of global issues Global citizenship	Understanding situatedness Addressing divisive but key contemporary issues Multiple identity positionings Reduction of stereotypes and humanisation of 'other' Activation
Risks/Limitations	Methodological nationalism Banal nationalism Superficial engagement Illusion of commonality Mainly global north partnerships Reluctance to engage in divisive topics	Focus on solution, limited time for interpersonal exchange/intercultural learning Reinforcing national identity through training materials Unequal power dynamics due to language and country of origin prejudice Reproducing coloniality (white saviour syndrome) Neoliberal functionalist approach to intercultural communication English language dominance	Video communication not accessible to all Risks of negative group dynamics and not feeling heard Difficult to ensure quality of facilitators English language dominance Power dynamics

Europe and the Southern Mediterranean Area) project which comprises engagement with content, ten weekly dialogue sessions and collaboration on a climate-related project. However, it is important to point out, that in neither case is the group project the main objective of the exchange, the focus remains on the dialogue process rather than a final product.

In the context of the Erasmus+ Virtual Exchange pilot project in which four different models of VE were implemented, a 'hybrid' model emerged which saw the integration of facilitated dialogue sessions in VEs that were based on cultural comparisons and problem- or challenge-based VEs. Dialogue sessions with trained facilitators were introduced at the outset of exchanges, in the middle and at the end (Helm & Velden, 2021). Generally, the first session was to ensure that participants got to know one another on a personal level, and they engaged in identity-related activities. In the middle of the exchanges, a session was held to monitor the progress of the exchange and the relations between participants, encouraging them to talk about dynamics within the group and to support the growth of a 'small group' culture. A final dialogue session was held at the end of the exchange, in order to allow for a collective reflection and debrief on the exchange and acknowledgement of participants' contributions to each other's intercultural learning.

6.1 What Next?

This Element began with a brief history of VE which included two projects developed to address geopolitical issues of the time, the New York/Moscow Schools Telecommunications Project, which began at the end of the Cold War and then the Soliya Connect Program which addressed relations between United States and predominantly Arab and Muslim world in the wake of 9/11. It is ironic and tragic that at the time of writing this Element, Russia's war in Ukraine has passed the two-year mark, and three months ago the Israeli government launched an unprecedented attack on Gaza and in three months has killed over 30,000 people and over 70,000 injured.[49] Across the globe, anti-semitism, Islamophobia and xenophobia are on the rise.[50] Whilst people are filling the streets with demonstrations showing support for and solidarity with Palestinians, it appears that dialogue about what is happening is being stifled in higher education as scholars and students are being monitored, disciplined, and expelled from institutions[51] and scholars engage in self-censorship in fear

---

[49] https://reliefweb.int/report/occupied-palestinian-territory/hostilities-gaza-strip-and-israel-flash-update-125.

[50] www.ohchr.org/en/press-releases/2023/11/un-human-rights-chief-condemns-rise-hatred.

[51] https://universitiesireland.ie/scholars-at-risk-ireland-issue-statement-regarding-the-ongoing-conflict-in-israel-palestine/.

of retaliation.[52] There is a lack of brave spaces (Glimäng, 2022), that is spaces where people can engage in dialogue about divisive topics, even amongst scholars and institutions whose main concern is intercultural communication. Yet the need for intercultural dialogue and the identification and interrogation of coloniality is high, given the increasing dehumanisation of the other and the strong push back against the contextualisation of recent events in histories of coloniality and repression.

Calls to decolonise education and knowledge are being taken up in various fields, including intercultural communication and global citizenship education, foreign language education and social sciences and are beginning to make their way into the field of VE (Banerjee et al., 2023; Guimarães & Finardi, 2021; Wimpenny et al., 2022). Souza and Duboc problematise intercultural dialogue in relation to decolonial pedagogies and point to the need for praxis, conceptualised as 'practice with conceptual reflection' (2021, p. 878). What they suggest is that before or when engaging in practice and implementation, theories and concepts of decolonial theory need to be engaged with and appreciated, practice is not enough. Furthermore, they propose three strategies for interrupting coloniality: 'thinking communication otherwise', 'bringing the body back', and 'marking the unmarked'. These are explained as follows:

> Thinking communication otherwise involves going beyond a focus on dialogue and problematizing universal presuppositions about interlocutors in a dialogue, such as, they are equal and equally human, and that the language of the dialogue is complete, neutral, transparent and nonconflictual. Bringing the body back involves rejecting and going beyond the modern presupposition of universality as produced by the separation of body from mind, rationality from emotion, and universal from local. Marking the unmarked goes beyond the presupposition of universal normativity to unleash a plurality of possibly conflicting normativities. (Souza & Duboc, 2021, p. 882)

I believe that VE has potential for thinking communication otherwise and for engaging with interculturality from a more critical, political, and decolonial perspective. It entails, as Souza and Duboc (2021) suggest, educators and students engaging with theories of coloniality, with previously excluded knowledges and histories, and juxtaposing them with the forms of knowledge we are familiar with. This means recognising histories and inequalities, different levels of humanness, that is, the 'colonial difference', acknowledging and addressing complicities, which is neither easy nor comfortable. It means letting go of certainties, unlearning in order to relearn.

---

[52] www.haaretz.com/us-news/2023-12-06/ty-article/.premium/growing-number-of-u-s-based-mid east-scholars-self-censoring-after-oct-7-hamas-attack/0000018c-3eb9-d826-ab9e-bfbfcc820000.

References

Abrahamse, A., Johnson, M., Levinson, N., et al. (2015). A virtual educational exchange: A north–south virtually shared class on sustainable development. *Journal of Studies in International Education*, *19*(2), 140–159. https://doi.org/10.1177/1028315314540474.

Adams, M. (2021). Comparative disciplines: An introduction. In M. Adams & M. V. Hoecke, eds., *Comparative methods in law, humanities and social sciences*. Cheltenham: Edward Elgar, pp. 1–10.

Agar, M. (1994). *Language shock: Understanding the culture of conversation.* New York: William Morrow.

Akkari, A., & Maleq, K. (2020). *Global citizenship education: Critical and international perspectives.* Cham: Springer.

Al Mqadma, A., & Al Karriri, A. (2020). Erasmus+ virtual exchange for internationalisation in besieged areas: A case study of the Islamic University of Gaza. In F. Helm & A. Beaven, eds., *Designing and implementing virtual exchange – a collection of case studies.* Dublin/Voillans: Research-publishing.net, pp. 167–178. https://doi.org/10.14705/rpnet.2020.45.1124.

Alami, N., Albuquerque, J., Ashton, L., et al. (2022). Marginalization and underrepresentation in virtual exchange: Reasons and remedies. *Journal of International Students*, *12*(S3), 57–76.

Alcoff, L. (2011). An epistemology for the next revolution. *TRANSMODERNITY: Journal of Peripheral Cultural Production of the Luso-Hispanic World*, *1*(2), 67–78. https://doi.org/10.5070/T412011808.

Allport, G. W. (1954). *The nature of prejudice.* Cambridge, MA: Addison-Wesley.

Andreotti, V., & de Souza, L. M. T. M. (2008). Translating theory into practice and walking minefields: Lessons from the project 'through other eyes'. *International Journal of Development Education and Global Learning*, *1*, 23–36. https://doi.org/10.18546/IJDEGL.01.1.03.

Andreotti, V., & Souza, L. M. M. de (Eds.). (2014). *Postcolonial perspectives on global citizenship education.* New York: Routledge.

Appel, H. B., Martínez-Fernández, M. C., & Fernández-Martínez, E. (2023). Implementation of COIL in mental health education: Outcomes of a collaboration between Spain and the United States nursing students. *Journal of Virtual Exchange*, *6*, 65–82. https://doi.org/10.21827/jve.6.39836.

Argo, N., Idriss, S., & Fancy, M. (2009). *Media and intergroup relations: Research on media and social change.* Dubai: Soliya and the United Nations

Alliance of Civilizations. https://dokumen.tips/documents/media-and-inter group-relations-research-on-media-and-social-change.html.

Avgousti, M. I. (2018). Intercultural communicative competence and online exchanges: A systematic review. *Computer Assisted Language Learning, 31* (8), 819–853. https://doi.org/10.1080/09588221.2018.1455713.

Bagga-Gupta, S. (2023). Epistemic and existential, E2-sustainability. On the need to un-learn for re-learning in contemporary spaces. *Frontiers in Communication, 8.* www.frontiersin.org/journals/communication/articles/ 10.3389/fcomm.2023.1081115/full.

Bagga-Gupta, S., & Dahlberg, G. M. (2021). On studying peoples' participation across contemporary timespaces: Disentangling analytical engagement. *Outlines. Critical Practice Studies, 22,* 49–88. https://doi.org/10.7146/ocps .v22i.125861.

Baker, W. (2015). *Culture and identity through English as a Lingua Franca: Rethinking concepts and goals in intercultural communication.* Berlin: De Gruyter Mouton.

Baker, W. (2022). *Intercultural and transcultural awareness in language teaching.* Cambridge: Cambridge University Press (Elements in Language Teaching).

Banerjee, S., Shaw, D., & Sparke, M. (2023). Collaborative online international learning, social innovation and global health: Cosmopolitical COVID lessons as global citizenship education. *Globalisation, Societies and Education,* 1–14. https://doi.org/10.1080/14767724.2023.2209585.

Barbosa, M. W., & Ferreira-Lopes, L. (2023). Emerging trends in telecollabora- tion and virtual exchange: A bibliometric study. *Educational Review, 75*(3), 558–586. https://doi.org/10.1080/00131911.2021.1907314.

Baroni, A., Dooly, M., Garcés García, P., et al. (2019). *Evaluating the impact of virtual exchange on initial teacher education: A European policy experiment.* Research-publishing.net. https://doi.org/10.14705/rpnet.2019.29.97824900 57337.

Baroni, A. & Helm, F. (forthcoming). Virtual exchange as a pedagogy of listening and of possibilities. In J. Z. Martinez & K. Silva, eds., *Entre diálogos, sensibilidades e aprendizagens: os múltiplos chapéus de Lynn Mario Trindade Menezes de Souza.* Campinas: Mercado de Letras.

Beaven, A., & Borghetti, C. (2016). Interculturality in study abroad. *Language and Intercultural Communication, 16*(3), 313–317. https://doi.org/10.1080/ 14708477.2016.1173893.

Beelen, J., & Jones, E. (2015). Redefining internationalization at home. In A. Curaj, L. Matei, R. Pricopie, J. Salmi, & P. Scott, eds., *The European higher education area: Between critical reflections and future policies*. Cham: Springer, pp. 59–72.

Belz, J. A. (2002). Social dimensions of telecollaborative foreign language study. *Language Learning & Technology*, *6*(1), 60–81.

Belz, J. A., & Thorne, S. L. (2006). *Internet-mediated intercultural foreign language education*. Boston, MA: Thomson Heinle.

Belz, J., & Vyatkina, N. (2005). Learner corpus analysis and the development of L2 pragmatic competence in networked inter-cultural language study: The case of German modal particles. *Canadian Modern Language Review*, *62*(1), 17–48. https://doi.org/10.3138/cmlr.62.1.17.

Benini, S., Giralt, M., & Murray, L. (2022). Global citizenship and virtual exchange practices: Promoting critical digital literacies and intercultural competence in language education. In C. Lütge, T. Merse, & P. Rauschert, eds., *Global citizenship in foreign language education*. New York: Routledge, pp. 151–173.

Bennett, J. M. (Ed.). (2015). *The Sage encyclopedia of intercultural competence*. Los Angeles, CA: SAGE.

Bhabha, H. K. (1994). *The location of culture*. New York: Routledge.

Bhambra, G. K., Gebrial, D., & Nişancıoğlu, K. (Eds.). (2018). *Decolonising the university*. London: Pluto Press.

Billig, M. S. (1995). *Banal nationalism*. Los Angeles, CA: Sage.

Block, D. (2007). *Second language identities*. London: Continuum.

Bourne, D. (Ed.). (2020). *The Bloomsbury handbook of global education and learning*. London: Bloomsbury.

Bowen, K., Barry, M., Jowell, A., Maddah, D., & Alami, N. H. (2021). Virtual exchange in global health: An innovative educational approach to foster socially responsible overseas collaboration. *International Journal of Educational Technology in Higher Education*, *18*(32), 1–11. https://doi.org/10.1186/s41239-021-00266-x.

Brooks, R., Courtois, A., Faas, D., Jayadeva, S., & Beech, S. (2024). International student mobility within Europe: Responding to contemporary challenges. *Higher Education*. https://doi.org/10.1007/s10734-024-01222-0.

Bruneau, E., Hameiri, B., Moore-Berg, S. L., & Kteily, N. (2020). Intergroup contact reduces dehumanization and meta-dehumanization: Cross-sectional, longitudinal, and quasi-experimental evidence from 16 samples in five countries. *Personality and Social Psychology Bulletin*, *47*(6), 906–920. https://doi.org/10.1177/0146167220949004.

Bruneau, E., & Saxe, R. (2012). The power of being heard: The benefits of 'perspective-giving' in the context of intergroup conflict. *Journal of*

Experimental Social Psychology, *48*(4), 855–866. https://doi.org/10.1016/j.jesp.2012.02.017.

Bruni, T. (2020). Integrating Soliya's connect programmes into a language course and into a liberal arts and sciences degree. In F. Helm & A. Beaven, eds., *Designing and implementing virtual exchange – a collection of case studies*. Research-publishing.net, pp. 205–216. https://doi.org/10.14705/rpnet.2020.45.1127.

Burbules, N. C. (2006). Rethinking dialogue in networked spaces. *Cultural Studies ↔ Critical Methodologies*, *6*(1), 107–122. https://doi.org/10.1177/1532708605282817.

Byram, M. (1997). *Teaching and assessing intercultural communicative competence*. Clevedon: Multilingual Matters.

Byram, M. (2008). *From foreign language education to education for intercultural citizenship: Essays and reflections*. Clevedon: Multilingual Matters. https://doi.org/10.21832/9781847690807.

Carolin, A., & Johnson, L., C. (2023). *Final Report – Transnational Virtual Exchange for Social Justice Education*. www.stevensinitiative.org/wp-content/uploads/2023/05/Stevens-Initiative-Sponsored-Research-Final-Report-Transnational-Virtual-Exchange-for-Social-Justice-Education.pdf.

Castillo, T. I. L., King, L. F. E., & Ruíz, L. P. Á. (2021). El intercambio virtual: Experiencias desde instituciones en el Caribe colombiano. *Edutec. Revista Electrónica de Tecnología Educativa*, *75*, 90–109. https://doi.org/10.21556/edutec.2021.75.1893.

Chun, D. M. (2011). Developing intercultural communicative competence through online exchanges. *CALICO Journal*, *28*(2), 392–419. https://doi.org/10.11139/cj.28.2.392-419.

Chun, D. M. (Ed.). (2014). *Cultura-inspired intercultural exchanges: Focus on Asian and Pacific languages*. National Foreign language Resource Center (NFLRC): University of Hawai'i at Mānoa.

Chun, D. M. (2015). Language and culture learning in higher education via telecollaboration. *Pedagogies: An International Journal*, *10*(1), 5–21. https://doi.org/10.1080/1554480X.2014.999775.

Çiftçi, E. Y., & Savaş, P. (2018). The role of telecollaboration in language and intercultural learning: A synthesis of studies published between 2010 and 2015. *ReCALL*, *30*(3), 278–298. https://doi.org/10.1017/S0958344017000313.

Cioltan-Drăghiciu, A., & Stanciu, D. (2020). Virtual exchange: Romania and Hungary 100 years later. In F. Helm & A. Beaven, eds., *Designing and implementing virtual exchange – a collection of case studies*. Research-publishing.net, pp. 37–46. https://doi.org/10.14705/rpnet.2020.45.1113.

Cogburn, D. L., & Levinson, N. S. (2008). Teaching globalization, globally: A 7-year case study of South Africa–U.S. virtual teams. *Information Technologies and International Development*, *4*(3), 75–88. https://doi.org/10.1162/itid.2008.00018.

Cogburn, D., Levinson, N., Ramnarine-Rieks, A., & Espinoza Vasquez, F. (2010). A decade of globally distributed collaborative learning: Lessons learned from cross-national virtual teams. *43rd Annual Hawaii International Conference on System Sciences*, Honolulu, HI, USA, pp.1–11. https://doi.org/10.1109/HICSS.2010.11.

Cole, T. (2012, March 21). The White-Savior Industrial Complex. *The Atlantic*. www.theatlantic.com/international/archive/2012/03/the-white-savior-industrial-complex/254843/.

Colpaert, J. (2020). Editorial position paper: How virtual is your research? *Computer Assisted Language Learning*, *33*(7), 653–664. https://doi.org/10.1080/09588221.2020.1824059.

Couldry, N., & Mejias, U. A. (2023). The decolonial turn in data and technology research: What is at stake and where is it heading? *Information, Communication & Society*, *26*(4), 786–802. https://doi.org/10.1080/1369118X.2021.1986102.

Cummins, J., & Sayers, D. (1997). *Brave new schools: Challenging cultural illiteracy through global learning networks*. Gordonsville, VA: Palgrave Macmillan.

Darvin, R. (2016). Language and identity in the digital age. In S. Preece, ed., *The Routledge handbook of language and identity*. Abingdon: Routledge, pp. 523–540.

Darvin, R., & Norton, B. (2015). Identity and a model of investment in applied linguistics. *Annual Review of Applied Linguistics*, *35*, 36–56. https://doi.org/10.1017/S0267190514000191.

Darvin, R., & Sun, T. (2024). Intercultural communication and identity. Cambridge: Cambridge University Press (*Elements in Intercultural Communication*). https://doi.org/10.1017/9781009206754.

Deardorff, D. K. (Ed.). (2009). *The Sage handbook of intercultural competence*. Thousand Oaks, CA: Sage.

Deardorff, D. (2022). Communicating successfully across differences within COIL virtual exchange. In J. Rubin & S. P. Guth, eds., *The guide to COIL virtual exchange*. Sterling, VA: Stylus, pp. 274–286.

Dooly, M. (2008). *Telecollaborative language learning*. Bern: Peter Lang.

Dooly, M., & O'Dowd, R. (2018). *In this together: Teachers' experience with transnational, telecollaborative language learning projects*. Bern: Peter Lang.

Dooly, M., & Sadler, R. (2013). Filling in the gaps: Linking theory and practice through telecollaboration in teacher education. *ReCALL*, *25*(01), 4–29. https://doi.org/10.1017/S0958344012000237.

Dooly, M., & Vinagre, M. (2022). Research into practice: Virtual exchange in language teaching and learning. *Language Teaching*, *55*(3), 392–406. https://doi.org/10.1017/S0261444821000069.

Dovchin, S., Pennycook, A., & Sultana, S. (2018). *Popular culture, voice and linguistic diversity: Young adults on- and offline*. Cham, Switzerland: Springer.

Ely, R. J., & Thomas, D. A. (2020, November 1). Getting serious about diversity: Enough already with the business case. *Harvard Business Review*. https://hbr.org/2020/11/getting-serious-about-diversity-enough-already-with-the-business-case.

European Commission. (2023). *Europe on the move – A proposal on the future of learning mobility | European Education Area*. https://education.ec.europa.eu/node/2736.

Ferri, G. (2018). *Intercultural communication*. Cham, Switzerland: Springer. https://doi.org/10.1007/978-3-319-73918-2.

Ferri, G. (2022). The master's tools will never dismantle the master's house: Decolonising intercultural communication. *Language and Intercultural Communication*, *22*(3), 381–390. https://doi.org/10.1080/14708477.2022.2046019.

Freire, P. (1970). *Pedagogy of the oppressed*. London: Penguin Books.

Fuchs, C. (2019). Critical incidents and cultures-of-use in a Hong Kong-Germany telecollaboration. *Language Learning & Technology*, *23*(3), 74–97.

Furstenberg, G., & English, K. (2016). Cultura revisited. *Language Learning & Technology*, *20*(2), 172–178.

Furstenberg, G., Levet, S., English, K., & Maillet, K. (2001). Giving a virtual voice to the silent language of culture: The Cultura project. *Language Learning & Technology*, *5*(1), 55–102. https://doi.org/10125/25113.

Gallagher, S. E., & Savage, T. (2023). Challenge-based learning in higher education: An exploratory literature review. *Teaching in Higher Education*, *28*(6), 1135–1157. https://doi.org/10.1080/13562517.2020.1863354.

Garcìa, J. S., & Crapotta, J. (2007). Models of telecollaboration (2): Cultura. In R. O'Dowd, ed., *Online intercultural exchange: An introduction for foreign language teachers*. Clevedon: Multilingual Matters, pp. 62–84.

Giralt, M. (2020). Communication across cultures: When the virtual meets the classroom. In F. Helm & A. Beaven, eds., *Designing and implementing virtual exchange – a collection of case studies.* Research-publishing.net, pp. 191–203. https://doi.org/10.14705/rpnet.2020.45.1126.

Giralt, M., Bets, A., Pittarello, S., & Stefanelli, C. (2022). Scenarios for the integration of virtual exchange in higher education. *Journal of International Students, 12*(S3), 116–134. https://doi.org/10.32674/jis.v12iS3.4629ojed.org/jis.

Glimäng, M. R. (2022). Safe/brave spaces in virtual exchange on sustainability. *Journal of Virtual Exchange, 5*, 61–81. https://doi.org/10.21827/jve.5.38369.

Godar, S., & van Ryssen, S. (2022). A brief history of global virtual teams. In V. Taras, ed., *The X-culture handbook of collaboration and problem solving in global virtual teams.* Greensboro: UNC Greensboro University Libraries, pp. 1–8.

Godwin-Jones, R. (2019). Telecollaboration as an approach to developing intercultural communication competence. *Language Learning & Technology, 23* (3), 8–28.

Grosfoguel, R. (2015). Epistemic racism/sexism, westernized universities and the four genocides/epistemicides of the long sixteenth century. In M. Araújo & S. R. Maeso, eds., *Eurocentrism, racism and knowledge: Debates on history and power in Europe and the Americas.* London: Palgrave Macmillan, pp. 23–46.

Guilherme, M., & Souza, L. M. M. de. (2019). *Glocal languages and intercultural critical awareness.* New York: Routledge.

Guimarães, F. F., & Finardi, K. R. (2021). Global citizenship education (GCE) in internationalisation: COIL as alternative thirdspace. *Globalisation, Societies and Education, 19*(5), 641–657. https://doi.org/10.1080/14767724.2021.1875808.

Guth, S., & Helm, F. (2017). *SUNY COIL Stevens Initiative Assessment FINAL REPORT.* https://doi.org/10.13140/RG.2.2.35940.27529.

Hall, E. T. (1990). *The silent language.* New York: Anchor Books.

Hantrais, L. (2008). *International comparative research: Theory, methods and practice.* New York: Bloomsbury.

Hauck, M. (2019). Virtual exchange for (critical) digital literacy skills development. *European Journal of Language Policy, 11*(2), 187–210.

Hauck, M. (2023). From virtual exchange to critical virtual exchange and critical internationalization at home. *The Global Impact Exchange*, 9–12.

Hauck, M., Müller-Hartmann, A., Rienties, B., & Rogaten, J. (2020). Approaches to researching digital-pedagogical competence development in VE-based teacher education. *Journal of Virtual Exchange, 3*, 5–35. https://doi.org/10.21827/jve.3.36082.

Heleta, S., & Chasi, S. (2022). Rethinking and redefining internationalisation of higher education in South Africa using a decolonial lens. *Journal of Higher Education Policy and Management*, *45*(3), 261–275. https://doi.org/10.1080/1360080X.2022.2146566.

Heleta, S., & Chasi, S. (2024). Curriculum decolonization and internationalization: A critical perspective from South Africa. *Journal of International Students*, *14*(2), 75–90. https://doi.org/10.32674/jis.v14i2.6383.

Heleta, S., & Jithoo, D. (2023). International research collaboration between South Africa and rest of the world: An analysis of 2012–2021 trends. *Transformation in Higher Education*, *8*(0), 1–11. https://doi.org/10.4102/the.v8i0.246.

Helm, F. (2013). A dialogic model for telecollaboration. *Bellaterra Journal of Teaching & Learning Language & Literature*, *6*(2), 28–48. https://doi.org/10.5565/rev/jtl3.522.

Helm, F. (2015). The practices and challenges of telecollaboration in higher education in Europe. *Language Learning & Technology*, *19*(2), 192–217. https://doi.org/10125/44424.

Helm, F. (2016). Facilitated dialogue in OIE. In R. O'Dowd & T. Lewis, eds., *Online intercultural exchange: Policy, pedagogy, practice*. Abingdon: Routledge, pp. 150–172.

Helm, F. (2017). Critical approaches to online intercultural language education. In S. L. Thorne & S. May, eds., *Language, education and technology, 3rd ed.* New York: Springer, pp. 219–231.

Helm, F. (2018a). *Emerging identities in virtual exchange*. Dublin/Voillans: Research-publishing.net.

Helm, F. (2018b). The long and winding road . . . . *Journal of Virtual Exchange*, *1*, 41–63.

Helm, F. (2021). Dialogue facilitation: Learning to listen. In T. Beaven & F. Rosell-Aguilar, eds., *Innovative language pedagogy report*. Research-publishing.net, pp. 11–15. https://doi.org/10.14705/rpnet.2021.50.1229.

Helm, F., & Acconcia, G. (2019). Interculturality and language in Erasmus+ virtual exchange. *European Journal of Language Policy*, *11*(2), 211–233.

Helm, F., Baroni, A., & Acconcia, G. (2023). Global citizenship online in higher education. *Educational Research for Policy and Practice*, *23*, 1–18. https://doi.org/10.1007/s10671-023-09351-6.

Helm, F., & Guth, S. (2010). The multifarious goals of Telecollaboration 2.0: Theoretical and practical implications. In S. Guth & F. Helm, eds., *Telecollaboration 2.0: Language, literacies and intercultural learning in the 21st century*. Bern: Peter Lang, pp. 69–106.

Helm, F., Guth, S., & Farrah, M. (2012). Promoting dialogue or hegemonic practice? Power issues in telecollaboration. *Language Learning & Technology*, *16*(2), 103–127.

Helm, F., & Hauck, M. (2022). Language, identity and positioning in virtual exchange. In L. Klimanova, ed., *Identity, multilingualism and CALL: Responding to new global realities*. Sheffield: Equinox, pp. 24–48.

Helm, F., & Velden, B. van der. (2021). *Erasmus+ virtual exchange: Intercultural learning experiences: 2020 impact report*. Publications Office of the European Union. https://data.europa.eu/doi/10.2797/870428.

Himelfarb, S. (2014, January 2). The Real eHarmony. *Foreign Policy*. https://foreignpolicy.com/2014/01/02/the-real-eharmony/.

Himelfarb, S., & Idriss, S. (2011). *Exchange 2.0* (272). United States Institute for Peace. www.usip.org/sites/default/files/Exchange2.0.pdf.

Hobsbawm, E. (1996). The stories my country told me. Arena, BBC. www.youtube.com/watch?v=OyO2hbvxx8s&t=5s.

Hoecke, M. V. (2021). Comparing across societies and disciplines. In M. Adams & M. V. Hoecke, eds., *Comparative methods in law, humanities and social sciences*. Cheltenham: Edward Elgar, pp. 221–245.

Hofstede, G. (2001). *Culture's consequences: Comparing values, behaviors, institutions and organizations across nations*. Thousand Oaks, CA: Sage.

Holliday, A. (1999). Small cultures. *Applied Linguistics*, *20*(2), 237–264. https://doi.org/10.1093/applin/20.2.237.

Holliday, A. (2011). *Intercultural communication and ideology*. Los Angeles, CA: Sage.

Holliday, A. (2020). Culture, communication, context, and power. In J. Jackson, ed., *The Routledge handbook of language and intercultural communication*, 2nd ed. London: Routledge, pp. 39–54.

Hua, Z. (ed.). (2015). *Research methods in intercultural communication: A practical guide*, 1st ed. Hoboken, NJ: Wiley.

Hua, Z. (2018). *Exploring intercultural communication: Language in action*, 2nd ed. London: Routledge.

Icaza Garza, R., & Vázquez, R. (2018). Diversity or decolonization? Researching diversity at the university of Amsterdam. In G. K. Bhambra, D. Gebrial., & K. Nişancıoğlu, eds., *Decolonising the university*. London: Pluto Press, pp. 108–128. https://library.oapen.org/handle/20.500.12657/25936.

Imperiale, M. G. (2021). Intercultural education in times of restricted travel: Lessons from the Gaza Strip. *Intercultural Communication Education*, *4*(1), 22–38. https://doi.org/10.29140/ice.v4n1.446.

Imperiale, M. G., Phipps, A., & Fassetta, G. (2021). On online practices of hospitality in higher education. *Studies in Philosophy and Education, 40*(6), 629–648. https://doi.org/10.1007/s11217-021-09770-z.

Inglehart, R. (Ed.). (2003). *Human values and social change: Findings from the values surveys.* Leiden: Brill.

Jack, G., Phipps, A., & Arriaga, O. B. (2020). Intercultural communication in tourism. In J. Jackson, ed., *The Routledge handbook of language and intercultural communication*, 2nd ed. London: Routledge, pp. 535–551.

Jackson, J. (2018). Intervening in the intercultural learning of L2 study abroad students: From research to practice. *Language Teaching, 51*(3), 365–382. https://doi.org/10.1017/S0261444816000392.

Jackson, J. (2020). Introduction and overview. In J. Jackson, ed., *The Routledge handbook of language and intercultural communication*, 2nd ed. London: Routledge, pp. 1–15.

Jiménez, A. Bayraktar, S., & Taras, V. (2022). Learning to collaborate across borders: Insights from the X-culture project and the emergence of global virtual teams. In A. M. Palma & R. C. Brotons, eds., *International education narratives. Transdisciplinary educative innovation experiences based on bilingual teaching.* Ed. France: University of Burgos, pp. 99–108.

Jithoo, D. (2020). The contribution of virtual engagement. In *Study South Africa – The guide to South African higher education*, 19th ed. South Africa: IEASA, pp. 11–12. https://ieasa.studysa.org/wp-content/uploads/2021/01/SSA-19th-edition-final-artwork_compressed.pdf.

Jones, R. H., & Hafner, C. A. (2021). Online cultures and intercultural communication. In R.H. Jones & C.A. Hafner, eds., *Understanding digital literacies*, 2nd ed. Abingdon: Routledge, pp. 161–182.

Joris, M., Simons, M., & Agirdag, O. (2022). Citizenship as competence, what else? Why European citizenship education policy threatens to fall short of its aims. *European Educational Research Journal, 21*(3), 484–503. https://doi.org/10.1177/1474904121989470.

Karabati, S. (2022). Theories of virtual teams, international teams, and global virtual collaboration. In V. Taras, ed., *The X-culture handbook of collaboration and problem solving in global virtual team.* Greensboro: UNC Greensboro University Libraries, pp. 21–31.

Kern, R. (2014). Technology as Pharmakon: The promise and perils of the internet for foreign language education. *The Modern Language Journal, 98* (1), 340–357. https://doi.org/10.1111/j.1540-4781.2014.12065.x.

Kern, R., Ware, P., & Warschauer, M. (2004). Crossing frontiers: New directions in online pedagogy and research. *Annual Review of Applied Linguistics, 24*, 243–260. https://doi.org/10.1017/S0267190504000091.

Khoo, S., Mucha, W., Pesch, C., & Wielenga, C. (2020). Epistemic (in)justice and decolonisation in higher education: Experiences of a crosssite teaching project. *Acta Academica, 52*(1), 54–75. https://doi.org/10.18820/24150479/aa52i1/sp4.

Kim, J., Merrill, K., Xu, K., & Sellnow, D. D. (2020). My teacher is a machine: Understanding students' perceptions of AI teaching assistants in online education. *International Journal of Human–Computer Interaction, 36*(20), 1902–1911. https://doi.org/10.1080/10447318.2020.1801227.

King de Ramirez, C. (2021). Global citizenship education through collaborative online international learning in the borderlands: A case of the Arizona–Sonora Megaregion. *Journal of Studies in International Education, 25*(1), 83–99. https://doi.org/10.1177/1028315319888886.

King Ramírez, C. (2020). Influences of academic culture in collaborative online international learning (COIL): Differences in Mexican and U.S. students' reported experiences. *Foreign Language Annals, 53*(3), 438–457. https://doi.org/10.1111/flan.12485.

Kramsch, C., & Thorne, S. (2002). Foreign language learning as global communicative practice. In D. Block & D. Cameron, eds., *Globalization and language teaching*. London: Routledge, pp. 83–100.

Ladegaard, H. J., & Phipps, A. (2020). Intercultural research and social activism. *Language and Intercultural Communication, 20*(2), 67–80. https://doi.org/10.1080/14708477.2020.1729786.

Lamy, M., & Goodfellow, R. (2010). Telecollaboration and learning 2.0. In S. Guth & F. Helm, eds., *Telecollaboration 2.0: Language, literacies and intercultural learning in the 21st Century*. Bern: Peter Lang, pp. 107–138.

Lederach, J. P. (1995). *Preparing for peace: Conflict transformation across cultures*. Syracuse, NY: Syracuse University Press.

Lederach, J. P. (2003). Conflict transformation. In G. Burgess & H. Burgess, eds., *Beyond intractability*. Boulder, CO: Conflict Information Consortium. www.beyondintractability.org/essay/transformation.

Leeds-Hurwitz, W. (2010). Writing the intellectual history of intercultural communication. In T. K. Nakayama & R. T. Halualani, eds., *The handbook of critical intercultural communication*, 1st ed. Chichester: Wiley, pp. 21–33. https://doi.org/10.1002/9781444390681.ch2.

Leone, P. (2022). *Teletandem. Apprendere le lingue in telecollaborazione*. Cesena: Caissa Italia.

Levine, G., & Phipps, A. (Eds.). (2012). *Critical and intercultural theory and language pedagogy*. Boston, MA: Heinle, Cengage Learning.

Macfadyen, L. P., Roche, J., & Doff, S. (2004). *Communicating across cultures in cyberspace: A bibliographical review of intercultural communication online*. Münster: LIT.

Magi Educational Services. (1992). *Evaluation of the New York State/Moscow schools telecommunications project*. https://iearn.org/assets/general/NY_State_Moscow_Evaluation.pdf.

Malmqvist, J., Rådberg, K. K., & Lundqvist, U. (2015). Comparative analysis of challenge-based learning experiences. *Proceedings of the 11th International CDIO Conference, Chengdu University of Information Technology, Chengdu, Sichuan, P.R. China, June 8–11*.

Marginson, S. (2022). What is global higher education? *Oxford Review of Education*, *48*(4), 492–517. https://doi.org/10.1080/03054985.2022.2061438.

Martin, G. S., & Crichton, J. (2020). Intercultural communication in health care settings. In J. Jackson, ed., *The Routledge handbook of language and intercultural communication*, 2nd ed. London: Routledge, pp. 503–520.

Meyer, E. (2014). *The culture map: Breaking through the invisible boundaries of global business*. New York: PublicAffairs.

Mignolo, W. (2002). The geopolitics of knowledge and the colonial difference. *The South Atlantic Quarterly*, *101*(1), 57–96.

Mignolo, W. D. (2012). *Local histories/global designs: Coloniality, subaltern knowledges, and border thinking*. Princeton, NJ: Princeton University Press. https://doi.org/10.23943/princeton/9780691156095.001.0001.

Nagda, B. (Ratnesh) A., & Gurin, P. (2007). Intergroup dialogue: A critical-dialogic approach to learning about difference, inequality, and social justice. *New Directions for Teaching and Learning*, *2007*(111), 35–45. https://doi.org/10.1002/tl.284.

NICE (2020). *The NICE programme: Your roadmap to starting virtual exchange*. Edinburgh: University of Edinburgh. https://edglobal.egnyte.com/dl/kKzQCHKLIH.

Nolte-Laird, R. (2022). *Peacebuilding online: Dialogue and enabling positive peace*. Singapore: Springer. https://doi.org/10.1007/978-981-16-6013-9.

Odeny, B., & Bosurgi, R. (2022). Time to end parachute science. *PLoS Med*, *19*(9), 1–3, e1004099. https://doi.org/10.1371/journal.pmed.1004099.

O'Dowd, R. (2006). *Telecollaboration and the development of intercultural communicative competence*. Munich: Langenscheidt.

O'Dowd, R. (Ed.). (2007). *Online intercultural exchange: An introduction for foreign language teachers*. Clevedon: Multilingual Matters.

O'Dowd, R. (2018). From telecollaboration to virtual exchange: State-of-the-art and the role of UNICollaboration in moving forward. *Journal of Virtual Exchange*, *1*, 1–23. https://doi.org/10.14705/rpnet.2018.jve.1.

O'Dowd, R. (2020). A transnational model of virtual exchange for global citizenship education. *Language Teaching*, *53*(4), 477–490. https://doi.org/10.1017/S0261444819000077.

O'Dowd, R. (2021). Virtual exchange: Moving forward into the next decade. *Computer Assisted Language Learning, 34*(3), 209–224. https://doi.org/10.1080/09588221.2021.1902201.

O'Dowd, R. (2023). *Internationalising higher education and the role of virtual exchange.* Abingdon: Routledge.

O'Dowd, R., & Dooly, M. (2020). Intercultural communicative competence development through telecollaboration and virtual exchange. In J. Jackson, ed., *The Routledge handbook of language and intercultural communication.* London: Routledge, pp. 361–375.

O'Dowd, R., & Lewis, T. (2016). *Online intercultural exchange: Policy, pedagogy, practice.* Abingdon: Routledge. https://doi.org/10.4324/9781315678931.

O'Dowd, R., & Ritter, M. (2006). Understanding and working with 'failed communication' in telecollaborative exchanges. *CALICO Journal, 23*(3), 623–642.

O'Dowd, R., & Ware, P. (2009). Critical issues in telecollaborative task design. *Computer Assisted Language Learning, 22*(2), 173–188.

OECD. (n.d.). *Global competence – PISA.* Retrieved 30 November 2023, from www.oecd.org/pisa/innovation/global-competence/.

OECD. (2018). *Preparing our youth for an inclusive and sustainable world: The OECD PISA global competence framework.* Paris: OECD. https://www.oecd.org/content/dam/oecd/en/topics/policy-sub-issues/global-competence/Handbook-PISA-2018-Global-Competence.pdf.

Olsen, J., Zimmer, A., & Behr, M. (2006). Real success with a virtual exchange: The German and American politics electronic classroom. *PS: Political Science & Politics, 39*(02), 351–355. https://doi.org/10.1017/S1049096506060562.

O'Rourke, B. (2007). Models of telecollaboration (1): eTandem. In R. O'Dowd, ed., *Online intercultural exchange: An introduction for foreign language teachers.* Clevedon: Multilingual Matters, pp. 41–61.

Ortega, L., & Zyzik, E. (2008). Online interactions and L2 learning: Some ethical challenges for L2 researchers. In S. S. Magnan, ed., *AILA applied linguistics series*, Vol. 3, Amsterdam: John Benjamins, pp. 331–355.

Pais, A., & Costa, M. (2020). An ideology critique of global citizenship education. *Critical Studies in Education, 61*(1), 1–16. https://doi.org/10.1080/17508487.2017.1318772.

Panina, D. (2022). Focusing on culture in X-culture. In V. Taras, ed., *The X-culture handbook of collaboration and problem solving in global virtual teams.* Greensboro: UNC Greensboro University Libraries, pp. 75–86. https://doi.org/10.5149/9781469669809_Taras.

Paolini, S., Harwood, J., Hewstone, M., & Neumann, D. L. (2018). Seeking and avoiding intergroup contact: Future frontiers of research on building social integration. *Social and Personality Psychology Compass*, *12*(12), 1–19, e12422. https://doi.org/10.1111/spc3.12422.

Pennycook, A. (2007). The myth of English as an international language. In S. Makoni & A. Pennycook, eds., *Disinventing and reconstituting languages*. Clevedon: Multilingual Matters.

Piller, I. (2016). *Linguistic diversity and social justice: An introduction to applied sociolinguistics*. Oxford: Oxford University press.

Phillipson, R. (1992). *Linguistic imperialism*. Oxford: Oxford University Press.

Piller, I. (2017). *Intercultural communication: A critical introduction*, 2nd ed. Edinburgh: Edinburgh University Press.

Porto, M., Houghton, S. A., & Byram, M. (2018). Intercultural citizenship in the (foreign) language classroom. *Language Teaching Research*, *22*(5), 484–498. https://doi.org/10.1177/1362168817718580.

Quijano, A. (2000). Coloniality of power and eurocentrism in Latin America. *International Sociology*, *15*(2), 215–232. https://doi.org/10.1177/0268580900015002005.

Ramírez, C. K. (2022). Virtual exchange in Latin America: A profile of faculty and staff participants. *Journal of Virtual Exchange*, *5*, 105–132. https://doi.org/10.21827/jve.5.38284.

Rampazzo, L., & Cunha, J. N. C. (2021). Telecollaborative practice in Brazil: What has been published about teletandem? *BELT – Brazilian English Language Teaching Journal*, *12*(1), e40023–e40023. https://doi.org/10.15448/2178-3640.2021.1.40023.

Richter, N. F., Martin, J., Hansen, S. V., Taras, V., & Alon, I. (2021). Motivational configurations of cultural intelligence, social integration, and performance in global virtual teams. *Journal of Business Research*, *129*, 351–367. https://doi.org/10.1016/j.jbusres.2021.03.012.

Rings, G., & Rasinger, S. M. (2022). *The Cambridge introduction to intercultural communication*, 1st ed. Cambridge: Cambridge University Press. https://doi.org/10.1017/9781108904025.

Rubin, J., & Guth, S. P. (Eds.). (2022). *The guide to COIL virtual exchange*. Sterling, VA: Stylus.

Rubin, J., Wimpenny, K., Portillo, B. G., et al. (2022). Taking coil virtual exchange to scale: 2004 to 2020. In J. Rubin & S. Guth, eds., *The guide to COIL virtual exchange*. Sterling, VA: Stylus, pp. 152–184.

Santos, B. de S. (2014). *Epistemologies of the south: Justice against epistemicide*, 1st ed. London: Routledge.

Satar, M., Hauck, M., & Bilki, Z. (2023). Multimodal representation in virtual exchange: A social semiotic approach to critical digital literacy. *Language Learning & Technology*, *27*(2), 72–96.

Saunders, H. H. (1999). *A public peace process: Sustained dialogue to transform racial and ethnic conflicts*, 1st ed. New York: St. Martin's Press.

Saunders, H. (2001). The virtue of sustained dialogue among civilizations. *International Journal on World Peace, 13*(1), 35–44.

Schneider, J., & Emde, von der, S. (2006). Conflicts in cyberspace: From communication breakdown to intercultural dialogue in online collaborations. In J. A. Belz & S. L. Thorne, eds., *Internet-mediated intercultural foreign language education*. Boston, MA: Thomson Heinle, pp. 178–206.

Schratz, M. (2014). The European Teacher: Transnational perspectives in teacher education policy and practice. *Center for Educational Policy Studies Journal, 4*(4), 11–27. https://doi.org/10.26529/cepsj.183.

Schröder, U., Adami, E., & Dailey-O'Cain, J. (Eds.). (2023). *Multimodal communication in intercultural interaction*. London: Routledge.

Schultz, K. (2003). *Listening: A framework for teaching across differences*. New York: Teachers College Press.

Schumann, S., & Moore, Y. (2022). What can be achieved with online intergroup contact interventions? Assessing long-term attitude, knowledge, and behaviour change. *Analyses of Social Issues and Public Policy, 22*(3), 1072–1091. https://doi.org/10.1111/asap.12333.

Scollon, R., & Scollon, S. B. K. (2001). *Intercultural communication: A discourse approach*, 2nd ed. Malden, MA: Blackwell.

Shahjahan, R. A., Estera, A. L., Surla, K. L., & Edwards, K. T. (2022). 'Decolonizing' curriculum and pedagogy: A comparative review across disciplines and global higher education contexts. *Review of Educational Research, 92*(1), 73–113. https://doi.org/10.3102/00346543211042423.

Sindoni, M. G. (2023). Multimodality and translanguaging in video interactions. *Elements in applied linguistics*. Cambridge: Cambridge University Press. https://doi.org/10.1017/9781009286947.

Sorrells, K. (2020). Social justice, diversity, and intercultural – global citizenship education in the global context. In J. Jackson, ed., *The routledge handbook of language and intercultural communication*, 2nd ed. London: Routledge, pp. 376–394.

Souza, L. M. T. M. de. (2019). Glocal languages, coloniality and globalization from below. In M. Guilherme & L.M.T.M. de Souza, eds., *Glocal languages and critical intercultural awareness*. New York: Routledge, pp.17–41.

Souza, L. M. T. M. de, & Duboc, A. P. M. (2021). De-universalizing the decolonial: Between parentheses and falling skies. *Gragoatá, 26*(56), 876–911. https://doi.org/10.22409/gragoata.v26i56.51599.

Souza, L. M. M. de. (2022). Internationalization: On cosmopolitanism, cosmo-politics and communication otherwise. *Critical Internationalization Studies Masterclass*. www.youtube.com/watch?v=YVSG550MiAg.

Spivak, G. C. (1999). *A critique of postcolonial reason: Toward a history of the vanishing present*. Cambridge, MA: Harvard University Press. https://doi.org/10.2307/j.ctvjsf541.

Starke-Meyerring, D., & Wilson, M. (2008). *Designing globally networked learning environments: Visionary partnerships, policies, and pedagogies*. Rotterdam: Sense.

Stein, S., & de Andreotti, V. O. (2016). Cash, competition, or charity: International students and the global imaginary. *Higher Education*, *72*(2), 225–239. https://doi.org/10.1007/s10734-015-9949-8.

Stevens Initiative. (2021). Virtual Exchange Typology. www.stevensinitiative.org/resource/virtual-exchange-typology/.

Stevens Initiative. (2024). *2024 Survey of the Virtual Exchange Field Report*. www.stevensinitiative.org/resource/2024-survey-of-the-virtual-exchange-field-report/.

Symeonidis, V., & Impedovo, M. A. (2023). Where internationalisation and digitalisation intersect: Designing a virtual exchange to enhance student teachers' professional awareness as European teachers. *European Journal of Teacher Education*, *46*(5), 821–839. https://doi.org/10.1080/02619768.2023.2243644.

Taras, V. (2022a). Known problems in GVTs and best ways to address them: The X-culture experience. In V. Taras, ed., *The X-culture handbook of collaboration and problem solving in global virtual teams*. Greensboro: UNC Greensboro University Libraries, pp. 162–175.

Taras, V. (Ed.). (2022b). *The X-culture handbook of collaboration and problem solving in global virtual teams*. Greensboro: UNC Greensboro University Libraries. https://doi.org/10.5149/9781469669809.

Taras, V., Rowney, J., & Steel, P. (2009). Half a century of measuring culture: Review of approaches, challenges, and limitations based on the analysis of 121 instruments for quantifying culture. *Journal of International Management*, *15*(4), 357–373. https://doi.org/10.1016/j.intman.2008.08.005.

Taras, V., Steel, P., & Stackhouse, M. (2023). A comparative evaluation of seven instruments for measuring values comprising Hofstede's model of culture. *Journal of World Business*, *58*(1), 1–11, 101386. https://doi.org/10.1016/j.jwb.2022.101386.

Tavoletti, E., & Kochkina, N. (2022). Dealing with ethnocentrism in global virtual teams. In V. Taras, ed., *The X-culture handbook of collaboration and problem solving in global virtual teams.* Greensboro: UNC Greensboro University Libraries, pp.102–117.

Tavoletti, E., Stephens, R. D., Taras, V., & Dong, L. (2022). Nationality biases in peer evaluations: The country-of-origin effect in global virtual teams. *International Business Review, 31*(2), 1–13, 101969. https://doi.org/10.1016/j.ibusrev.2021.101969.

Tavoletti, E., & Taras, V. (2023). From the periphery to the centre: A bibliometric review of global virtual teams as a new ordinary workplace. *Management Research Review, 46*(8), 1061–1090. https://doi.org/10.1108/MRR-12-2021-0869.

Telles, J. A., & Vassalo, M. L. (2006). Foreign language learning In-Tandem: Teletandem as an alternative proposal in CALLT1. *The ESPecialist, 27*(2), 189–212. https://revistas.pucsp.br/index.php/esp/article/view/1629.

Thorne, S. L. (2016). Cultures-of-use and morphologies of communicative action. *Language Learning & Technology, 20*(2), 185–191. http://dx.doi.org/10125/44473.

Train, R. (2006). A critical look at technologies and ideologies in internet-mediated intercultural foreign language education. In J. A. Belz & S. L. Thorne, eds., *Internet-mediated intercultural foreign language education.* Boston, MA: Thomson, Heinle, pp. 247–284.

Train, R. (2012). Postcolonial complexities in foreign language education and the humanities. In G. Levine & A. Phipps, eds., *Critical and intercultural theory and language pedagogy.* Boston, MA: Heinle Cengage Learning, pp. 141–160.

Trompenaars, A., & Hampden-Turner, C. (1997). *Riding the waves of culture: Understanding cultural diversity in business,* 2nd ed. London: Nicholas Brealey.

Tyszblat, R. (2019). Taking dialoghe online. In S. Gruener, S. Smith, & M. Hald, eds., *Dialogue in peacebuilding: Understanding different perspectives.* Uppsala: The Dag Hammarskjöld Foundation, pp. 179–187.

UNESCO. (2014). *Global citizenship education: Preparing learners for the challenges of the twenty-first century.* Paris: UNESCO. https://unesdoc.unesco.org/ark:/48223/pf0000227729.

Uvarov, A. Yu. , & Prussakova, A. A. (1992). The international telecommunication project in the schools of Moscow and New York State. *Educational technology research and development, 40*(4), 111–118.

Walsh, C. E. (2018). Interculturality and decoloniality. In W. D. Mignolo & C. E. Walsh, eds., *On decoloniality.* New York: Duke University Press, pp. 57–80. https://doi.org/10.1515/9780822371779-005.

Ware, P. (2005). 'Missed' communication in online communication: Tensions in a German-American telecollaboration. *Language Learning & Technology, 9*(2), 64–89.

Ware, P., & Kramsch, C. (2005). Toward an intercultural stance: Teaching German and English through telecollaboration. *The Modern Language Journal, 89*(2), 190–205.

Warschauer, M. (1995). *Virtual connections: Online activities & projects for networking language learners.* Honolulu, HI: University of Hawai'i press.

Wilkinson, J. (2012). The intercultural speaker and the acquisition of intercultural/global competence. In J. Jackson, ed., *The Routledge handbook of language and intercultural communication.* London: Routledge, pp. 283–298.

Williams, R. (1985). *Keywords: A vocabulary of culture and society* (Rev. ed). New York: Oxford University Press.

Wimpenny, K., Finardi, K. R., Orsini-Jones, M., & Jacobs, L. (2022). Knowing, being, relating and expressing through third space global south-north COIL: Digital inclusion and equity in international higher education. *Journal of Studies in International Education, 26*(2), 279–296. https://doi.org/10.1177/10283153221094085.

Yoo, B., Donthu, N., & Lenartowicz, T. (2011). Measuring Hofstede's five dimensions of cultural values at the individual level: Development and validation of CVSCALE. *Journal of International Consumer Marketing, 23*(3–4), 193–210. https://doi.org/10.1080/08961530.2011.578059.

Yuan, M., Dervin, F., Liang, Y., & Layne, H. (2023). 'Just take your time and talk to us, okay?' – International education students facilitating and promoting interculturality in online initial interactions. *British Journal of Educational Studies, 71*(6), 637–661. https://doi.org/10.1080/00071005.2023.2231526.

Zwerg-Villegas, A. M., & Martínez-Díaz, J. H. (2016). Experiential learning with global virtual teams: Developing intercultural and virtual competencies. *Magis. Revista Internacional de Investigación En Educación, 9*(18), 129–146.

Cambridge Elements ☰

Intercultural Communication

Will Baker
University of Southampton

Will Baker is Director of the Centre for Global Englishes and an Associate Professor of Applied Linguistics, University of Southampton. His research interests are Intercultural and Transcultural Communication, English as a Lingua Franca, English medium education, Intercultural education and ELT, and he has published and presented internationally in all these areas. Recent publications include: *Intercultural and Transcultural Awareness in Language Teaching (2022)*, co-author of *Transcultural Communication through Global Englishes (2021)*, co-editor of *The Routledge Handbook of English as a Lingua Franca (2018)*. He is also co-editor of the book series 'Developments in English as Lingua Franca'.

Troy McConachy
University of New South Wales

Troy McConachy is Senior Lecturer in the School of Education at University of New South Wales. His work aims to make interdisciplinary connections between the fields of (language) education and intercultural communication, focusing particularly on the role of metapragmatic awareness in intercultural communication and intercultural learning. He has published articles in journals such as ELT Journal, Language Awareness, Intercultural Education, the Language Learning Journal, Journal of International and Intercultural Communication, Journal of Intercultural Communication Research, and others. His is author of the monograph *Developing Intercultural Perspectives on Language Use: Exploring Pragmatics and Culture in Foreign Language Learning* (Multilingual Matters), and he has co-edited *Teaching and Learning Second Language Pragmatics for Intercultural Understanding* (with Tony Liddicoat), and *Negotiating Intercultural Relations: Insights from Linguistics, Psychology, and Intercultural* Education (with Perry Hinton). He is also Founding Editor and former Editor-in-Chief (2017-2024) of the international journal Intercultural Communication Education (Castledown).

Sonia Morán Panero
University of Southampton

Sonia Morán Panero is a Lecturer in Applied Linguistics at the University of Southampton. Her academic expertise is on the sociolinguistics of the use and learning of English for transcultural communication purposes. Her work has focused particularly on language ideologies around Spanish and English as global languages, English language policies and education in Spanish speaking settings and English medium instruction on global education. She has published on these areas through international knowledge dissemination platforms such as ELTJ, JELF, *The Routledge Handbook of English as a Lingua Franca* (2018) and the British Council.

About the Series

This series offers a mixture of key texts and innovative research publications from established and emerging scholars which represent the depth and diversity of current intercultural communication research and suggest new directions for the field.

Cambridge Elements $^{\equiv}$

Intercultural Communication

Elements in the Series

A full series listing is available at: www.cambridge.org/EIIC

Printed in the United States
by Baker & Taylor Publisher Services